Spiritual Stretches

Volume One

An Inner Evolution

Karen Barker

Copyright © 2007 by Karen Barker

ISBN 0-7414-3663-9

Photos by Ed Barker, Willy Fuder, Bill Clifford and Karen Barker

Artwork done by Aly and Karen Barker

Cover Design and Photo by Lee Simmons "Indian Paintbrush"

Published by:

PUBLISHING.COM

1094 New DeHaven Street, Suite 100
West Conshohocken, PA 19428-2713
Info@buybooksontheweb.com
www.buybooksontheweb.com
Toll-free (877) BUY BOOK
Local Phone (610) 941-9999
Fax (610) 941-9959

Printed in the United States of America

Printed on Recycled Paper

Published January 2007

Dedication

To all my Spiritual Teachers who picked me up, shone the light so bright that it guided me home and to all those who are open to receive.

Acknowledgments

With heartfelt gratitude to Willy Fuder, Alycia Barker, Lyn Inglis, Red Hawk and Jay Paul whose patience and support over this time is appreciated.

I would also extend this same blessing to the Development Groups over 2001-2004, whose commitment to being all they can be in this lifetime has brought a deeper understanding to my purpose, for we have been each others teachers.

To my unseen friends of energy and light who have come forward with their love and compassion bringing a deeper peace and healing to my life.

Blessings to those who journey into this book, may you find direction and insight knowing you are spiritual beings having a physical experience.

Comments on the profound impact of *Spiritual Stretches*

I loved the 'Spiritual Stretches' – they help energize my soul.

**Fiona Nicholson,
President of Contact Works/Life coach**

This has given me tools to develop my intuition and somehow awakened a watchfulness for the beauty and grace in life. Thank you for stepping out in light and love, best of luck with the destination of this beautiful message.

Barbara Eastham, Yoga Instructor

Karen initiates by example and in her book she lays the pathway to her heart *and* ours in open invite. The joy in her commitment to living in the present moment becomes ours as she shares steps that have worked for her. Karen holds a deep and honorable reverence for all life. This love is palpable in the words she writes. It is that love that ultimately moves us as we read. Karen walks her talk and through her gentle, yet passionate encouragement, we are led to have faith that we can, as well.

Kate Rogers

The first time I opened up *Spiritual Stretches*, I was in the car waiting for my son, JJ, and his friend while they were playing paintball. I felt a very powerful presence – I thought Archangel Michael? I saw a soft blue/grey color before Karen accurately described the color of dolphins. I did one of the exercises and felt so blissful and peaceful. The second time I opened up the book, JJ and I both smelled the Vibhuti that Amma manifests. It was a clearly experienced by both of us simultaneously. I understand that Karen writes about Amma in the book but I had not yet read that piece.

Mary Ann Hutchings

Table of Contents

Spiritual Stretches
Volume One
Index

Interview with Karen
January 11, 2005
Pages 37-72

Table of Contents
Spiritual Stretches
Volume Two
Index

Introduction

My hope is that in sharing these stretches one can go within to get re-connected with all of who we are and come to the realization that we are all interconnected and inter dependent in that spiritual understanding. Many times in this Third Dimension we reach for what is tangible because of our experience here on Earth. I, with love and compassion, share these spiritual stretches that reach inward to explore who we are within. For within ourselves is where the healing begins as we awaken to our fullest potential that we are all spiritual beings having a physical experience

Look at the colors of the rainbow. Beautiful as they are, each color of the rainbow vibrates to a different frequency, red being the lowest and violet being the highest vibration. The emotions reflect that same relationship in its full spectrum from fear to love. In healing the resistant energies, which act as obstacles in our lives, we create more space for love and light to be. As spiritual beings having a physical experience we need freedom to flourish. There is truth for the necessity to clean up the negative thought patterns in our life so that we can learn or remember to celebrate life with the joy filled celebration of being here.

These are a few stretches that have affected my life profoundly with their simplicity. I have done them as needed during the day and they have transformed my life into a Heaven on Earth. The illusion of living in pain and sickness has not served one of us. To experience home here on Earth is a deep peace that only the soul can know.

The Universe's expansive knowledge will embrace all who ask for it. It is like a veil that needs to be lifted and it is made available, for we are all one. Therefore the healing of duality and separation is integral within us and this world to evolve.

The cosmos and spiritual energies all aid in transmuting and transforming the density so we may rejoice in light to a life of peace and grace for all. The struggle will end and the love that surrounds us, which has been with us always, will now be felt and experienced.

In peace and unity, please join me in these simple ways of transforming or re-claiming the journey as divine beings that we all are.

Feeling Energy

As we begin, it is important to know we all can feel the energies around us. The wonderful feeling when you encounter something in Mother Nature that speaks to you like a beautiful tall tree you feel drawn to eat your lunch under on a sunlit day, the joy the gentle rain gives you as it dances off your skin or window pane wherever you may be. Being in a room with those you love, feeling the safety and peace it brings you as opposed to entering a room with a group of people you may not know and sensing who you feel drawn or safe to sit beside. For instance, as you wait in a doctor's office. These are all examples of how we use energy.

We all know what it feels like when we avoid sitting beside a person that gives us the "No feeling". In simple terms, you have just had an awareness of energies around you. All these observations are responses to energy.

A simple exercise to help you get a tangible experience of energy is, place your hands about 6 inches apart then bring them slowly together then apart. You may feel a tingling or some resistance as you bring them together and apart several times. That is your energy. We all have energy fields that surround us as well. When we feel heat from someone's hands as they touch us or hold a part of our physical body that is in pain, is a form of healing energy. It always will feel peaceful and comforting never invasive.

When my daughter was younger, I described it as having the "Yes feeling" or "No feeling" from someone. This gave her a simple vocabulary to share her thoughts or perceptions of people.

Start from this moment forward to incorporate this awareness in your daily life. Notice those that give you the

"Yes" or "No" feeling, knowing that your personal radar is communicating to you. The next part of the learning curve is to trust it. That is where healing the resistant energies will be useful as part of the steps of the journey in awakening the healing within.

We plant that seed, water it, and watch it grow. We learn about the plant. Be patient, for sometimes when the plant grows it is imperceptible. Trust in the process for the plant's stem will come, then the leaves, and in time, the flower.

Healing Resistant Energy/ Recycling Emotions

The resistant energies that we hold in our body or mind is like a contraction. It can create illness; make us feel unwell mentally. Clearing ourselves, acknowledging them in our patterns is the first step to be able to open fully in our hearts to listen. The denser energies, like fear, will attract the same vibration, fear.

It is time to awaken to different choices that will serve our highest purpose. Imagine what it would be like to experience joy, everyday of being alive. For some of us, it is a dream. For some of us, we have worked hard to be there. I am joy. On the Earth as we know it now, there are the denser energies that are playing out in magnitude. So I have great compassion with myself as a spiritual being in this physical experience for that. It seems hard to feel free.

The resistance is global and in humanity a thousand fold. This book is an awakening to choose differently. As we do our daily physical exercises, we can also incorporate our daily spiritual stretches to fully enhance ourselves. Be patient and compassionate with yourselves on your new journey as you evolve and grow.

The Dalai Lama makes reference to the fact that there is no word in the English language for self-compassion. If the journey starts within, the compassion needs to start from within.

I bless you on this journey. I ask the Universe for its love, protection and direction at all times.

Start allowing yourselves to bless everything that comes into your path or enters your consciousness. For example, bless the highway as it gets you to work, bless the bird, thoughts of poverty or struggle, bless the joy, bless the coffee, the chocolate, and the Soya milk. Allow yourself to be creative and witness how you see things start to change. Be playful.

A dear friend of mine, Lyn Inglis is a natural medium who received her certification in Portsmouth, England. An energy she channels is known to her and me, as Jay Paul. Over the last few years she has been an incredible teacher for me in developing my intuition. I will refer to her and Jay Paul through out this text, sharing the wonders they have so graciously shared with me. You will be introduced as well, to Dr. Steven Aung. Since 1996, I have experienced his guidance and healing work in my own personal recoveries. He has instructed me in Qi Gong. With his love and kindness he has inspired me with self healing meditations.

Jay Paul, advised me to clear the self-judgment and fear that was within me. It created obstacles in my ability to fully come into what is the next stage of my journey. He was very emphatic and I knew he was offering me some essential guidance. In retrospect, I wasn't sure how I was going to do it. He shared that in Spirit no energy judges another for their choices for it is all experience. Judgment has been created in humanity in the Third Dimensional frequency. The old dynamic that I was running was

3

negative thought processes causing huge contractions inside me, preventing the light and my personal growth.

I turned to Lyn who shared; in the moment, acknowledge the emotion, feel it for it is mine then send the energy up to my mind's eye where I can express my disappointment or frustration in having to work through this, yet again. After having owned the self-judgment in its entirety, I brought the energy into my heart surrounding it with love and compassion transforming the vibration which is what it felt like into a higher vibration love or compassion. Then exhale the whole experience. I would go inside again and see if it had truly gone or whether I had to do the whole process again.

In the beginning, I had to recycle this emotion once, twice or three times depending on my state. I had to cultivate self compassion in a disciplined way. Now after a few years of doing this, I can honestly say it comes as an involuntary response, when I experience any feelings that are lower in vibration.

So I ask you to do some searching as to what your resistant energies are and be diligent in transforming them because the reward is freedom. As Thich Nhat Hanh says, we are more than our feelings.

Sit in meditation stance in a quiet place and find the stillness. If you have a hard time letting an emotion go, for example, I feel...disappointment. Bring the emotion up to the mind's eye and say, "I am so tired of dealing with this, I am angry at his choice to send that controlling energy at me." As a spiritual being having this physical experience I have huge love and compassion for myself at having to experience this. I surround the energy with love as I say these words as I connect with my higher self. I then embrace my physical self, and exhale. I re-evaluate. If I feel at peace, I give thanks and bless the moment of peace. As I

4

breathe in, I feel peace, as I breathe out; I smile at my body's peace.

Resistant energies attract resistant energies. This is why it is so important we release them so the light and higher vibrational feelings such as love and kindness can be with us more frequently. Those higher vibrations attract higher vibrations. This is when we can start to see our world shift. The type of people we meet will start to change as we attract those that are more in tune with our interests. We may feel our job or wardrobe shifting because we desire from our hearts differently. I went from wearing black, navy, to colors that were brighter white, gold and blues. These hold the resonance of emotional healing. Allow this and bless the process knowing the work you are doing is serving you. Remembering energy is never wasted.

Virus and Bacteria

Virus and bacteria have been born and breed in the lower frequencies. In your meditation ask "to raise my frequency to the precise vibration so that virus or bacteria cannot live in my physical body". Virus and bacteria can only survive in the lower frequencies or the denser vibrations. It has its own purpose. We need to raise our level of understanding so that the virus and bacteria can not exist within us.

As Sam Graci writes in "Super foods" there is scientific evidence that thought, yoga, meditation can change the alkalinity in our bodies so we can be healthier. Acidity in our bodies causes joints to be arthritic and various other pathologies. Acidity can be nurtured by negative thoughts, foods; choices we make that do not serve our highest good. One can go into a health food store and purchase the test paper that Greens Plus makes which is a tool to analyze the urine in the morning for its acidity. It's great and tangible.

Keep pure thoughts by listening to music or singing mantras.

For example, the Dalai Lama always starts his day with, Ohm mane pad me ohm. Robert Thurman's book "Circling the Sacred Mountain" has a fabulous dissertation on the meaning of that mantra.

Try playing music that calms or clears uncomfortable energy. The sound of the Tibetan bowl or chanting "Ohm" is great to quickly shift the energies in your office or home. It clears or transforms the resistant energy.

Dr. Steven Aung, my Chi Gong teacher, referred to the exercise as "recycling of our emotions" or "emotional purification". The breath, which I will refer to often, is food, oxygen for the body. Without that component our body starts decaying.

Oxygenation, alkalinity are keys to transforming disease. Sam Graci talks about it in "Super foods" as well as many other sources. Lyn Inglis' guide, Jay Paul, whom she channels, has taught me a version of this as well. I have previously shared this with you but will review it.

Bless the emotion within. Raise it into the mind and acknowledge it. Breathe into the heart where it will receive love and compassion. Let that river of grace surround it, then exhale.

Dr. Steven Aung suggests that if you are out in nature, let the emotion go into the river for it will take it away and transform the negative energy into something positive. Also tree hugging is a great practice in Chi Gong. The tree is a conductor and will restore your battery with positive energy as it pulls the negative from you.

6

Giant Cedars, Revelstoke, B.C., Canada

That is why it weather permitting we love to sit under a tree and eat our lunch or write. Being out in nature always is healthy and inspirational. Find a sacred place that is easily accessible to you. It will be your retreat, a blessing and nature will love your company as well.

I have a funny story about a sacred place which taught me about transformation and letting go. I had a beautiful grandmother tree in a green space near my apartment. I went and sat at the base of its trunk and did my breathing meditations. It was in perfect alignment with the Three Sisters Mountains which has a healing vortex for the Earth that I have also visited. It connected me with that energy as I sat and journeyed.

Three Sisters, Canmore AB. Canada

There was a ferocious wind storm around Christmas one year. When the weather cleared, I went out to be with the grandmother and found she was the only one in this grove that had fallen. Emotionally I felt sad. Grieving for my loss, asking why, "She was the biggest, why her?"

I felt I was being punished. I had some work to do with these feelings. I connected with another tree that was there and realized she had taken over the grandmother duties. I sat with her for a while but felt too angry.

I did a ceremony in blessing the memories, planting some seeds at her base. As I started to feel with more clarity upon re-cycling my denser emotions, she was now to be host and home for many living things. I still visit her. The most beautiful experience I had was touching the top of the tree with the knowing I could never do that before. To feel the energy of her antenna was magnificent. She must have stood over 75 feet tall.

Sacred Heart Meditation

Journeying into the sacred heart is a great exercise, another gift from Jay Paul and Lyn. Enter into your heart connecting with how it feels today. Place your hand on it if you happen to have a hard time locating it. Many people cut themselves off from feeling because life has become very difficult. My compassion is with you.

As you connect breathe into the heart imagining the space between all the cells, the space is a brilliant light, the gold light of the Universe. As you breathe let the cells be suspended in the golden light that is there.

This is your connection with the Universe, your original self. When we have lost this connection we can easily loose our way, feel depressed, sad, and unbalanced. Allow yourself to fully practice being in this space until it becomes second nature or I should say until it becomes your original nature as you walk on the Earth.

Dream Collage

Make a collage of dreams and visions a positive focused activity that is tangible.

Affirmations

I am the light, I live in the light, I love the light, and I am protected, supported and provided for by the light. I bless the light.

I am God, I am Buddha, I am Narayani, Divine Mother of the Universe, I am Archangel Michael, I am Mother Mary, I am....(use any ascended masters or light beings that resonate with you)

I am that. Wait for the Universe to respond with, I am.

Focus using this phrase on all you see, it maybe other people, world situations, the beauty of the mountains etc. I found it was a challenge to embrace the denser energies as poverty and pain. After completing the first one, I realized in this exercise I was transmuting and transforming the denser energies. In trying this exercise, if fear presents itself, bless it and persevere.

It is all an illusion. This is an illusion. Look at the world around you and acknowledge that it is an illusion. Look at something specific and say it is an illusion. Pain is an illusion. It is all an illusion.

In the moment they present themselves offer up any frustrations or concerns, worries to the angels and God daily so they do not pollute your mind and the Earth.

It is done It is done It is done repeated three times is a declaration to the Universe that it is so.

Thank you God for this offering of love and in deep gratitude, be present to the deep profound thanks for all that is given to you.

Surround yourself with beauty and simplicity, as it is a mirror of who you truly are.

Visual Clutter

Clutter, visual clutter becomes a reflection for us. When we are choosing to see differently what we surround ourselves with is very important. Practice mindfulness when you choose to be surrounded by beauty or the color blue in your room. In doing these exercises you may find the need to change things in your environment, allow yourself to do that, as it is a reflection of your growth. Honor that.

Sing for healing

Sing your thoughts whenever the opportunity presents itself. For the voice and frequency begins inside. The cathedral of our mouths is directly related to the brain. Let that frequency travel and reverberate through out the brain and body out into your environment.

I love when my daughter chooses to sing in her baths. It is a wonderful reflection of her personal freedom of expression. The Soul and Spirit are united in song. Dr. Doreen Virtue author and psychologist who have created the term "Angel Therapy" says, where there are people singing, there are angels.

Her book entitled "Angel Medicine" journeys into the minerals of the Earth and her remembrances of healing in the time of Atlantis, where sound and frequency were primarily used for healings in the temples. The message from the Stonehenge Stones is that is very important that humanity reclaims their powers to heal themselves and to manifest.

Ask that ease and grace surrounds you and the joy filled celebration of being here graces you daily.

Meditation- Falls

In meditation stance, focus on your breath. Follow the pathway as it travels through your body, as it feeds and nourishes you consistently. If you have feelings acknowledge them as you breathe in and smile at them as you breathe out transforming them into a lighter frequency so you are clear to open your heart. For example, as I breathe in, I feel the anger inside me, as I breathe out I smile on my friend anger once again. As I breathe in I feel my heart racing, as I breathe out I smile to my racing heart. Work with this in the next 5 minutes to center yourself and to bring yourself into the present moment.

Thich Nhat Hanh's books and CD 'The Art of Mindfulness", teaches this beautiful and simple technique. You can purchase these at www.soundstrue.com or *www.plumvillage.com* which is his place of residence in France.

Chatterbox Falls, Princess Louisa Inlet, B.C

Now that you are there, look at the picture, acknowledging the way it makes you feel. See if you can project yourself into this beautiful place. Allow yourself to sit beside me on the rocks or find your own place to be. Open your heart to listen and feel the senses this invokes.

As you allow yourself to journey here frequently, each time it may take you into a deeper experience. Open yourself to that.

As you progress along, you can add: as I breathe in, I am the mountain as I breathe out, I am solid. Thich Nhat Hanh describes beautifully this positive imagery to invoke the strength and knowingness within us. The calmness is to be in the truth of the moment, to see clearly and lovingly with compassion for others who are struggling.

Practice Mindfulness.

Practice Mindfulness, is choosing to be consciously aware of all our actions, our choices, in thought, in our daily lives, at all times, in the present moment.

Re claiming our power

Have I inadvertently given my power away subconsciously? Has someone taken it? Why am I feeling unworthy, self doubting, small, empty?

From my experiences I have found sometimes that I have freely given away my power, my sense of self because of my nature or fear. Being in an abusive relationship be it a job related one or personal, the denser energies of control and manipulation can stifle our Spirit. For our Spirit needs freedom to be in its full expression. We have come into this Third Dimensional reality as Spirit with a physical limitation. We do not need any other limitation placed on us as in control or power. We will cover more regarding this concept later.

I had a spiritual teacher I journeyed with that served me for a time and I bless him. A time came where it dawned on me that I felt like a lamb and was struggling with the relationship. I lived in a different city so the distance gave me some clarity and space where I could come to the realization that I felt empty. This was not healthy. I was leaving my partner whom I had a child with, which was healthy. My teacher awoke me to that truth and I honor him, for it took courage to come to that place of decision to leave or let him know verbally that I did not love the situation I was in. I could not be truly who I was without him judging me. I would go to work and feel huge with energy but I knew that when I came home I made myself small and that saddened me. I know now that it was partly my self-judgment that he was reflecting, but I also knew it was part of my journey to move on.

I sat with the guidance of a friend and asked that my power come back to me from my teacher. All that I gave of my power I asked that it be returned to me now. I was still. All of a sudden it felt like a lightening bolt hit me. I was astonished at the response. It made me giggle for the first time in a while. "Oh there I am", I exclaimed. I felt in that instant quite different.

If you would like to try this, hold who it is that you are asking your power back from, call in the person's higher self and call out for all your power to return to you now. You may also address collective energies like the government, your religion, be creative and trust your divine inner voice. It is in responding and trusting the voice within that the deepest growth begins to happen. Have fun.

Clearing Energy

This is another energy technique for clearing external energies that pull us off our center affecting us emotionally, spiritually or physically.

As you are seated extend your focus or awareness outside the energy field surrounding your body. If you see or feel any strings pulling out from you acknowledges them as others or other energies pulling you off center and with love ask that the blue flaming sword of Archangel Michael cleanse and clearly cut these from you. As they are cut offer gratitude and send loving energy or ask Michael to send love in the direction of the string or cord. Surround yourself with violet and gold light from the Universe. Asking the Universe for its love, protection and direction at all times.

With regards to physical manifestation of pain, I have a place at the upper part of my back where it will ache and I see a hook in there at that level. I know exactly who it is because this person will not come around to the front and show themselves to me but like to inadvertently get my attention. I usually try to cut this attachment. If I still experience the physical pain, I will connect with this person's higher self asking them to call me on the phone if they need to talk. Very often this person within minutes will phone or I will receive a letter or email. If we can open our minds to that reality that our physical pain is energy we can start to move it with immediate results. It is very empowering when the physical pain goes instantly; it opens up in your mind a new growth and understanding that we are spiritual beings having a physical experience.

One may use Celtic sea salt or table salt which is also known as white light. It is a crystal and the denser energies can not be anchored when that is present. Sprinkle it around the perimeter of your home, at the windows or over your bed. I found with my daughter teaching her these simple ways empowered her. She felt more at peace, if she suffered from nightmares or didn't feel comfortable. Using candle light, flowers, minerals such as crystals and incense, they will anchor in the higher vibrations. Incense has a two fold purpose, as an offering and also in Chinese Medicine the herbs are inhaled through the lungs which can be beneficial for healing. That is why to use natural ingredients is so important or essential oils that are pure. These are affecting us physically as well.

These simple skills shared with our children are priceless. My daughter comes home after school and usually has a bath with incense or candlelight on her own initiative to help with clearing of all the energies she has encountered during the day, as well as to center herself.

Surround your home with the violet flame running constantly. This is a good clearing and protection technique. Take time and implement it around your child's school, office or local hospital.

Plants are wonderful. Some absorb negative energies, like the spider plant. One particular leaf of a spider plant, near my bed, would vibrate. The spider plant has hundreds of long leaves, so for one to vibrate, I paid attention. As soon as I would acknowledge it and connect with its meaning, it would instantly stop. It usually had a message for me with regards to increasing protective energy.

Flowering Plant Meditation

As an exercise, sit with a flowering plant that is not flowering at the time. See it as having flowers and know with your heart that the flowers are within this beautiful plant. Send it loving and compassionate energy holding the focus of the flowers. You may notice within a week the flowers will start to come. I have done this several times with the violets, jasmine plant and the wonderful Christmas cactus. If your plant is not healthy spent some time with it and look deeply as to what the cause maybe. It may want to be moved, put in sunlight for the afternoon or watered. They are sentient beings that are cohabitating with you. Honor them.

Receiving Meditation

Open your heart to receive all the beauteous and bountiful gifts the Universe has for you daily. Extend your arms in open posture and just say Yes repeatedly to the many gifts the Universe has for you.

Breathe in, acknowledging the breathing in and then experience the breathing out, knowing you are breathing out. With this single minded focus feel the gentleness of the breath moving your body, a wave like motion journeying deeper and deeper into yourself. Allow yourself to enjoy the peace and space, the gentleness and simplicity of this.

In this quiet moment, ask for support and direction so that you may be all that you can be in this journey and radiate your fullest potential out in the world. The frequency you carry is healing to all of those around you.

Reveal yourself and trust that God lives within you in every breath you take, for you are God and God is you and you are one. Your mind and the Godheads mind are one. The understanding that you share is profound and like a beacon transforms others on their journey to opening their hearts to the truth. For the truth spoken in any form or language is the truth for its frequency is truth.

Earth Healing Meditation

Hold your hands together feeling the energy that is created and imagine the globe of the Earth is between your hands. Then ask that the universal healing energies come through you to the Earth for healing. Open your heart to receive and listen then open your mind to be with the Earth.

Sun Meditation 1

Place a hand over your solar plexus and imagine the rays of the sun coming from your hand into your body, Enjoy. The rays then travel to the 4, 5, 6, and 7th chakra, out the top of your head to the sun. Let that circuit you have created run to clear and energize you.

Sun Meditation 2

On a sunny day, hold your palm to the nurturing sun and invite it in to every cell of your being. Say yes to it. Then hold it close to your heart as you breathe in its love and support for your journey. Breathe in the sun. With gratitude bless it for it fills your world with love and it is the true mother nurturing and sustaining life.

Clear the Listening Tube

Make sure the tube of listening is clear, an etheric tube that runs outside your body from the solar plexus to the Third eye. Connect by touching the solar plexus area then the Third eye to stimulate the connection and then imagine traveling down the tube. If it needs cleaning you will feel resistant energy or your hand will feel like it wants to stop. Visualize an etheric bottle brush, like you clean a baby bottle with and run it through the tube. Check the clarity of the connection as in the beginning of this exercise, with your hand touching your solar plexus to your Third eye between your eye brows. Sit in stillness working with the breath. Jay-Paul has taught me these things and it brings clarity to my journey when I do this exercise.

Tibetan bowls, Tinshaws or other instruments that create a high frequency are fabulous for clearing and centering of the energies that surround you. The sound will present itself differently in tone if there is denser energy. So with working in clearing and re balancing, listen with your human and etheric ear. Allow yourself to experience in your body the frequencies and sound. It will break up the lower frequencies not harmonious with you and then release them from your physical body.

In using my bowl to clear some energy on a client one day the energy came out of the bowl and physically grazed the side of my face. I felt it graze the side of my face like a comet of energy.

Creating a personal vortex

Place your hands in the stance where you are sending energy with your right hand and holding or receiving with your left hand. Your intention is to ask that you create a personal vortex of energy in your energy field that will serve you to harmonize and balance all your systems and provide you with a constant flow of universal healing energy. As you sit with the experience allow your self heart to be open to receive listen and open your mind to the images, colors, feelings you may experience.

Creating a Healing Vortex

Healing Vortex - At an area of vulnerability in your body create a smaller vortex asking the universal healings energies balance and heal the area. It may serve as a protection or buffer as it continually supplies healing energy until it no longer needs it.

Creating a group Vortex

A group vortex- Sitting in a circle as a group with hands facing towards the center of the circle ask that this vortex be created for the highest and greatest of all sentient beings. It will be fed by the constant work and growth of the group. It can be drawn on daily when needed by each participant at a distance. The energy is connected in at the solar plexus level.

If I am at home away from the group and want to call on this energy created for support, I go into that inner quiet place and visualize at my solar plexus a connection to the group vortex. It may appear as a flow of light or a tube. I breathe in, asking that this universal energy flow to nourish and rebalance my energy. Focusing on my breath I am open to receive. I give thanks, breathing in and out remembering to smile on the inside.

Three Sisters Healing Vortex, Canmore, AB, Canada

Lyn Inglis' **"Clear Light Meditation"** is fabulous for relaxation, learning to focus and feel other energies and frequencies. It is a channeled meditation by her guide Jay Paul, available at www.lyninglis.com.

Colors of the Rainbow Meditation

I am all the colors of the rainbow. Allow the breath to take you deeper into that understanding. Be present and take notice of any images, pictures, colors, feelings that you may have. Each of us receives and processes our messages differently. It is learning how you receive either in a clairaudient, clairsentient or visual medium.

The journey is discovering how you perceive.

Heal Yourself/Heal the Earth

There came a point in my healing work as a therapist when I was asking how I can serve to the highest and greatest good of all sentient beings. One day I just knew in my heart that if I healed myself I was healing the Earth. The work with each person that felt drawn to come into my office, I felt the same. I could picture them healed. I was holding that energy and vision in my heart. I knew that if I could create a space for them to heal I was helping the Earth heal. There was a peace within me. Clarity and acceptance of my journey evolved to a new level in my understanding of my work and being of service to others. I heal myself and so I heal the Earth.

I feel the Earth's energies of healing. Acknowledge the vibration of the Earth's movement and with the breath release the energy. For remember in essence, we are all energy and light, we can release and move the trapped energy within, therefore, the pain can go as well. Give yourself permission to experience this, as I have previously mentioned. A great majority of us on this planet have been disempowered to believe we can not heal or shift the pain we endure within ourselves. That is a thought that has held us in limitation.

Personal Healing with Crystals

Use Rose Quartz crystal as the mineral vibration of unconditional love to absorb any pain which is energy and send it to the furthest reaches of the Universe where it will be transformed. Release the energies into the quartz and give gratitude and thanks for this. Sometimes we need to invoke our unseen friends to hold extra energies for us to do this. I remember lying on my bed with a strong voice demanding help. In the moment the pain shifted. It was amazing and empowering for me.

Pink Bubble of Light

Very often I surround myself in a bubble of pink loving light which is a wonderful feeling. There are times that present themselves when I am with a person who is troublesome. It is an energy that is draining to be around. I will surround them in a pink bubble of energy and project them out into the atmosphere or Universe. Their energy towards me transforms into something I can work with or be around.

They will often respond with feeling not as connected to me. Some people will call or I will find that their behavior does not affect me in the same way; therefore, it is effortless to be around them.

The color pink is related to unconditional love. In my mind to be surrounded by that energy feels beautiful, an antidote for irritation. Try it with your pets or children when they are unwell or at unrest.

After the earthquake in South Asia there were waves of intense fear that traveled around the Earth, there was also the joy that followed the release as well. Bless the energy that was expressed by the Earth and all sentient life forms so that it may serve in the cleansing and healing rather than to cause death and destruction.

Other understandings we can open our minds to explore.

As we meet others we may feel that the drama playing out in our relationship with them seems old, repetitive or not of this lifetime. It may also feel that it is present but on another Dimension or world as we know it. Ask that it be shown to you so that it can be healed or that your understanding of the experience may be a conscious one. For that is where we are waking up to, that spiritual understanding of our physical experience, here on Earth. In this Third Dimensional limitation to express ourselves as fully as we can in Spirit, is our exercise. If it feels old, ask for clearing to release the old energy or residue past life energy in all directions of time and space, so that the relationship can be present in this lifetime.

I will present this perspective briefly and cover it in the next volume. Subconsciously, do we have resistances that are preventing us from being joyful or healing ourselves? There are the few clients that have shown me that they have psychological resistances around healing that may involve the desire not to be better. This energy has manifested in physical symptoms that need attention. Without judgment, they feel lost or lonely. Their power has been taken or given away unknowingly, and the sense of self is grasping for attention.

Deeply, I believe it is their way of asking for help. When someone is so off center that they are not able to identify the problem, it is up to us to shed some light to help them see their dynamic. I truly believe that if it is shown to me, I trust they are allowing on some level to reach for help. With love and compassion, I can help hold the energy of understanding for them, to come to a decision to seek help. We are all here for purpose. Being in the moment allows you to interact with what life gives you in that moment. No energy is wasted.

Expanding into who we truly are

Hold the space to choose different. Work with the vastness and expansiveness of our being. In the clear light meditation or working with the image of the sun is a start. Embrace yourself beyond the human minds definition of vastness into the infinite universal understanding of the expansiveness of who we all are.

New Teachers Blessing of Self Compassion

Whenever I feel limited or trapped in my physical form showing signs of quick breathing, anxiety, pain or panic, I remind myself to expand my conscious awareness. All of a sudden I start to feel better. It is like I have been holding myself in limitation and it is time to expand rather than hold my limited vision of the world, to move me forward. Whether the awareness comes to me driving in the car or in the shopping store, I take that time to expand and work with what presents itself in that moment.

A beautiful Japanese friend of mine, Clemie Hoshino, brought that concept forward to me in the 80's about addressing what life gives me in the moment so it didn't travel with me as baggage to do later. This has been amazing advice as it has kept me clearer and in the moment.

Being patient and compassionate with ourselves is important as we journey, for life's lessons are sometimes repetitive so we fully grasp the learning. Practice self compassion in this place. With deep gratitude, I send blessings to her.

Plant the seed with intention to serve you with the highest and the greatest good of all. It shapes the intention with clarity.

Watering Positive Seeds

Open the Heart

Listen

Open the mind

To the universal understanding that I am you, you are me, we are all one. With that understanding why would one desire to harm ourselves or others?

Gregg Braden and his wonderful words in his "Returning to Zero Point, A Collective Initiation," he acknowledges the word as a code and vibration in that higher understanding of how we process information. We are the information. All we need to know is within us. He has done some amazing work with DNA, emotion and the energies that surround them in communication. I have been aware or drawn to him and his work since 1996.

See yourself in all you meet.

Choose to say "Yes" to love, compassion in all things.

Choose to say "Yes" to see beauty in all things.

Choose to say "Yes" to see God, the divine, in all you meet.

Greatest Teachers are Adversity

What you would term your greatest enemy could be your greatest teacher in teaching you life lessons. I have always felt that I had big learning ahead when I sensed a sea of negativity approaching.

Since the beginning, I have felt my mother has been my biggest teacher. Allowing me to journey into the conscious purpose of that awareness was important for my personal growth. I know that she was there so I could choose different around what love is in my life, how it expresses itself. Thought is a powerful contributing factor to our well being.

Thought, I truly believe, if it could be seen or tangible would be like seeing Pig Pen on "Charlie Brown" walking around with the murky fog surrounding him. Thought is energy and choosing to think positive brings in the higher vibrations rather than the lower frequencies as we have explored through healing resistant energy.

Gregg Braden "Returning to Zero Point The Collective Initiation" and some of his other books have done research around the vibration of love opposed to hate lighting up more strands of our DNA when it was tested. I found that fascinating. There are huge healing attributes to cleaning up our thoughts and choosing the lighter brighter loving dialogue in our heads. Yes I can, I think I can, no, without a doubt **I know I can.**

Wishing our greatest teachers loving kindness on a daily basis will transform them or the situation, it maybe an effort but is definitely worth a try. Hold an image of them between your hands and send them love.

I had a learning experience where Revenue Canada had audited me over a two year period. Talk about an exercise of fear connected to authoritative figures, superiority and governments. It was a lesson in watching me give away my power habitually without question. I also became aware of the old paradigms we, as humanity had created.

I know I had served many lifetimes where I had been either burned at the stake or put in prison and tortured. That is the physical journey, for we are here to experience and be all things. Consciously, I was choosing to place my energy and intentions only for the greatest universal good of anchoring love and compassion, for humanity and the Earth. I made a conscious choice to hold the light so others may wakeup to that choice as well.

What I realized was I needed to hire an accountant so my energy would be freed up and refocused so I could help others more effectively. The old paradigms needed to be transformed. Most clearly for me was the awareness that people have been disempowered with respect to their rights.

I started studying the Magna Carta. It is in place to protect the rights of the common man from the government. I worked with those energies and it wasn't easy. I had physical heart palpitations when I worked through this journey. I placed loving intentions for the rebalancing of the dysfunctional energies.

Now, I can receive a letter from them and say "Oh, a letter from my friends" and not feel threatened or guilty. I needed to release and heal the negative projections and the wounded perceptions I was holding onto not only for myself but my compassion went out to humanity. What had we created!

The Wounded Perspective and Projections

Heal the wounded perspective and projections we create. Thich Nhat Hanh's books are fabulous for working with this concept. Two wonderful books that helped me and I refer to clients are, "Anger" and "No Fear, No Death".

Thought is instantaneous in Spirit; thought in the physical is energy that needs to be put in motion. A series of events need to happen to reach an outcome.

Welcome new experiences as teachers. Through all the surgeries that I have chosen to experience in my lifetime they have been my greatest teachers as well. I bless them for the knowledge and where this journey has taken me. I share and empower others now with that knowledge where fear can overtake them.

Create the space to allow for change. One technique I find helpful is I see myself stepping back as if out of my physical self. It creates the distance to see things a new and let go of the expectation of outcome. In stepping back out of myself it helps me let go.

As we anchor in the higher frequencies as love and compassion. It supports our new direction by infusing our thoughts therefore accommodating the shift in direction by influencing our choices. When we are spiritual beings having a physical experience choosing to love rather than be in fear we are closest to our original nature.

30

Busy-ness

If I am too busy how can beauty and peace make itself known to me. If busy-ness is a distraction in your life, the awareness has already come to you to ask the question, why am I creating this? The active lifestyle then becomes an obstacle or avoidance. Honor your awareness, be honest and truthful with yourself, journey with the breath into the "why" you have made those choices.

Addictions, Distractions and Toxic Choices

There are many blocks in the Third Dimension we have created to keep us from the truth. A few of these blocks can be identified as addictive behavior, toxins and ego. If you can ask for the authentic intention in this moment to let these obstacles go for the highest and greatest good of all, it is a start. Trust and believe in your intentions.

I am a single mother and self employed. I was going through a time where my love for red wine was a passion. I started to realize that I wasn't sleeping well at night, my attention was off and there were days where I felt sick for most of the following day. I knew for my highest good I needed to let this dependency go.

I didn't feel strong enough to do it by myself. I asked for my guides and the angelic realm to work with me to help me curb these experiences. I knew it wasn't serving me. It took me over 6 months floating in and out until now I can say that I will have a glass and sometimes it will just taste awful or yummy. When it tastes yummy, I will sit back and enjoy the glass of wine. When it doesn't, I will throw it down the sink and feel okay with that knowing it is for my highest good. I know in my heart I have set up that system with my guides and honor it.

Trust the universal energies that are supporting your journey for it is precious and sacred. Jay Paul always mentions this and adds that the human journey is a difficult one, but the learning curve is incredible and we are honored for it.

The Children in our lives are precious and sacred.

Our children are also our greatest teachers, for they will reflect what we need to heal within ourselves.

In the Indigos, their knowing is complete for they hold the energy of the future, the Fifth Dimensional frequency we all have lying in different stages within us. Some of us that have awoken to that remembering work with those children supporting their energy and purpose. Very often they know what they need.

Encourage them to join your breathing or meditations and ask them what they see. What colors you present to them as you journey into the clear light together. Ask your child to teach you to remember the truth. Honor them for their journey for being in a world that does not support their frequency is a difficult one.

There is a deep knowing within them that they will be taken care of, a frustration at the lack of justice monetarily distributed on the globe. I remember my daughter always saying everyone should have the same. There is enough. Money shouldn't be the way we live with each other.

Innately, she was expressing the old frequency needed to shift. They are also great manifesters. So team up with them to help them manifest what your dreams are together or what your journey together is about. By asking them to teach you, you empower and help them understand who they are and what their purpose is. Empowering them makes the light within them grow brighter to be all that they can in this lifetime. For they have great purpose.

A wonderful website www.emissaryoflight.com hosted by James Twyman and the beloved community out of Ashland, Oregon, has an internet course, "Reclaiming your Indigo Power". I have completed several of his Spiritual Peacemakers courses and they are supportive and enlightening. He has worked with many of these children. He has now teamed up with Neale Donald Walsch and Stephen Simon to produce the movies, "Indigo" and "The

Indigo Evolution". They both were released on January 29, 2005 and 2006 which is International Indigo day.

Karma is the rebalancing of energy.

When we choose to add to our karma we choose to act out of fear or anger. The result is most often destruction and pain for others. In this Fifth Dimensional understanding that these children hold karma does not exist. Making the choice to harm or cause pain to someone else is unthinkable. Harmony and balance will steer our decisions for ourselves and for the planet.

Support with love, our children's journey for it may seem uneasy, as they are a minority on the Earth planet now. A day will come when they will be of majority holding that frequency so love and peace will prevail.

Blessings to you all

All my needs are abundantly met now and forever. All my needs are abundantly met now and forever. I accept good graciously in my life. All my needs are abundantly met now and forever. It is so. It is so. It is so.

As my heart fills with the vibrancy of the electric alive pink January sunrise, the insight comes to me that this rainbow of color unfolds continually around the mother Earth planet. The energy of re birth and the joy filled celebration of the rainbow, liken it to a blanket of vibration, makes its way always somewhere on the Earth. That thought brings great joy and peace to me. I am seeing it all happen at a distance from the place of my original nature.

As you breathe in, know you are breathing in, then breathe out, know you are breathing out. As Thich Nhat Hanh refers to the Buddhist way and how this can bring you into the present moment, which is made up of the past and holds the unfolding of the future. So being in this present moment is where heaven on Earth lives and where life is.

Nurturing the seeds of happiness and ceasing the nurturing of the "not so" happy seeds will bring forth an awakened mind which is an aware mind. Mindfulness is the blood to go deeper into knowing. Being peaceful and calm allows the sun of truth to reveal the truth.

When emotional seeds are watered as in anger or jealousy, like a mother nurture them and they will transform. I am that....I am... We can be in a place of choosing which seeds we will nurture.

Be in the Moment

I keep hearing from my guides to be in the moment, just be in the moment and all will unfold. Trust in the beauty of the Universe that all our needs will be taken care of. Open the heart so it can feel and experience the truth. Do this and you will hold the energy for others to do so as well. We can call this "compassionate medicine."

In trusting you are in a place of listening with your heart and open mind so that the insights of the unfolding rainbow may bless you.

Communion with energy

Open your heart to come into communion with the energy you are embracing. I am referring to a loved one be it a pet or a person. Breathe into the moment, knowing you are breathing in with them in harmony. Breathing out, knowing you are breathing out in harmony feeling the energies merge and dance in celebration.

Pet Connection

My cat, Angel, is part of my spiritual family that has chosen to re-incarnate as a feline. She is close to me teaching me unconditional love so merging energies with her in unity is nothing to fear. In my life history and several past lives I have chosen difficult paths of abuse. Fear has been an energy that has taught me a lot about my power and will to transform the density. It has also taught me in knowing the density I have consciously chosen love and the light as my strength.

Angel and I enter into a place of bliss, and she so readily responds to the higher frequencies, when they come in as we go into that place of our original nature. She also lets me know when unseen beings enter the room or come to play with her by looking in their direction. As we speak, she is nestled across both my arms as I type these words, purring with peace. Breathing in, I know I am blessed, breathing out, I smile to that blessing. So work with your pet in this way and feel the deepening of that relationship grace your life. Telepathy will also be something that may open in your mind as well with that knowing.

I bless you for the journey you have shared with me. May you create that space to make some choices for a healthier you and a healthier planet? Empower yourself and your children with the knowing that you are spiritual beings having a physical experience.

Interview with Karen – January 11, 2005

At the time of this interview I was running two intuitive development groups with my good friend and colleague Lyn Inglis. A Psychiatrist in the group knew of a psychologist who was doing her masters on "Prayer and Healing." I went into that quiet place and felt drawn to connect with Barb. I called her and little did I know what beautiful a effect this would have on my healing journey.

A few days before our scheduled meeting, a place inside of me wanted to cancel the interview. I was feeling nervous and at a loss at what might come out. With mixed feelings I trusted in my first response of wanting to do this. That morning, I watched the sunrise and did some meditation of breathing with Thich Nhat Hanh. I arrived at my office about 15 minutes before to prepare.

I knew now all would unfold as it should be. "Trust" was my mantra.

In this time of adversity on the planet, it is so difficult to see the light. We are searching and wondering if there is a God with all the devastation and death. At this time we need to turn inside to discover the light within us that is our key to find our way out of the darkness or the hole we feel we are in.

This interview of my life experience is a support to those who are struggling.

My spiritual awareness was with me early in my life. Like the lotus, it is blossoming, clearing my resistant energies to be fully who I am in this physical experience. I feel blessed and honor all those who play a part in my journey. The grace and knowing that Spirit walks with us, not in front or behind us, is a comfort.

In this difficult time on this Earth where there is so much density playing out it is hard to feel supported by God, the angelic realm or Buddha at times. Having the discipline to meditate or pray in the face of adversity, when we are pulled off our center, is hard. I found I need the support of spiritual family. We are here as humanity to help each other.

Healing within, by addressing and clearing the resistant energies so we can listen with an open heart and open mind to all that is coming our way is who we are. We are spiritual beings in a physical experience.

The Universe is compassionate and ever present to our needs along this journey.

Blessings to you.

This interview takes place in Karen's office with Barb. Barb will be known as B and Karen is K.

B: I normally have begun these interviews with just a general opening up to invite you to talk about your experience with prayer as it connects to your life, specifically to health issues.

K: I came into this lifetime with congenital hip deformity. That was the start of my journey.

At the age of four months, I was a month in the hospital in traction without a lot of human touch. At that point in my life was when I was aware of my unseen friends, my angel partners and buddies. I just felt that my journey was going to be one of solitude, for a while.

Nine months after this experience, the doctors tried to put my hip back into place, I was then placed in a body cast which had rollers on it. Like a human surf board, I made my way around the floor. I was told by my mother, I always had a smile on my face.

B: At four months?

K: At four months old…yes. In my remembering, when I was ten days old, my mother, Nana and father went into their Roman Catholic Church and placed me on the altar. In this little wrapped bundle, they said in prayer, "Can you take care of her?" In that offering, that moment, I felt something happened to me.

I had moments in my life thinking, "Oh my God, how could they have done that?"

In retrospect, I know it was the greatest gift, because the journey through my lifetime has been with the Divine Mother energy of the Universe. I think very early in my life, I realized my mother was a universal being, and I was as well. We all are. The Divine Mother was *really* my mother and she was with me always. From that understanding, I started my spiritual journey. I think it was this innate knowing that I was…my energies was …more of a universal origin, if that makes sense.

My understanding at present is that I am a spiritual being having a physical experience.

I knew in my heart there was more than this physical life.

Only now in my life at forty-four, I really start to own it, talk and write about it to help others in their journey of pain.

At the age of five years old, I had my first major operation which brought me into a place of limitation, restriction, of judgment and all those feelings.

I was a devout child. I knew Jesus was my friend and loved to spend a lot of time in church. I was also exploring the desire of becoming a nun in my early teens. In time, I realized that wasn't my journey.

As I grew older because of the pain in my hips and the serious degeneration, I developed osteoarthritis. At the age of fourteen; I started becoming more immobilized on a physical level. I realized the journey of who I was, it was allowing my soul to fly, and I did that through prayer, through my faith.

I believe faith at the time to be the freedom of doubt and fear. I really found in that place, is where I lived. It brought me comfort amongst the physical pain.

I had a couple D and Cs. I felt quite connected to the energies that presented themselves. It was the circumstances of the events that I choose not to keep them. I have come to the understanding now, that it was the journey or the contract between me and those energies. Some energy chooses to experience gestation and part incubation, as part of their learning in Spirit. I do feel the energies present in my life at certain times.

When I was pregnant with Aly, my daughter, there was a certainty that this energy was coming to full term. I was told by my doctor that I shouldn't have children or warned it would be stressful physically. To my surprise, when I was pregnant, the energy was wonderful, so supportive. I felt the best in my lifetime, at thirty three.

I was working as a massage therapist; she would kick and touch some clients through my belly in a treatment. Those people are still present in our lives, even though we're physically not living in the same place. These people still have a very strong connection with her. It was her choosing them, in a way. One woman Aly kicked repeatedly in treatments, became her nanny.

The birth process for me was a challenge. I think, if it was fifty years ago, I probably would have passed over. My cervix dilated to 7 cms and would not open any more because my hips were fixed. We had a thirty three hour struggle in delivery which ended in a C-section. Previous to that, as they were giving me the drugs and epidurals my blood pressure crashed and that's when I had my near-death experience.

I came out of my body, all the noise, the machines and the beeping stopped. All I could hear was the nurse saying, "Her blood pressure has reached forty over twenty", something like that. As I heard that, everything went quiet. I don't know if you've ever sailed, what you call …parasailing…but you get up really high and it's just quiet. You don't hear anything…the birds, it's just surreal. That's what it felt like. I was in this cushion of energy and love and I could *feel* the energy of my Nana who was there when they placed me on the altar. She had died a few years ago. I turned to Aly's dad and I said, "She's come to get me. Nana's come to get me." I felt willing to go, because it felt so good, and two, I felt my life had been quite a struggle. I gave birth at the age of 33, which in reflection, is a significant number for me. I found out that it is the resonance of the Christ consciousness.

B: Mmm-hmm. Sorry, can you say more about that…the Christ consciousness?

K: Well thirty three, those numbers seem to be master numbers with regards to numerology. I don't know the science of it. Christ was 33 when he died. For me, when a master number comes into my life, I know I'm going in the right direction. 11:11, or 12:12 I have recently had an experience where that same number 33 was quite prevalent.

I pay attention. I try to really walk in my life with awareness. As Thich Nhat Hanh would say, or the Buddhists would say, **being alive is being in the present moment**. I pay attention and am mindful of all things and people that come in and out of my life and know there is purpose in that. I can feel those energies.

So, as I felt my energy lifting, in that place of bliss, peace and incredible love with my Nana…though I didn't see her, it was beautiful. She didn't physically manifest into form, but I knew she was with me. I felt I could have been there forever. All of a sudden, I became more conscious of the room, the sounds, the bells and I was aware I was back into my physical body, feeling the pain.

B: It sounds jarring….

K: Yes (laughter)…What I know is that as Spirit you don't have to deal with any of the emotional life we have in physical form. It's a difficult journey and I know we're honored for that. To be in that limitation, and to be fully in our Spirit in this physical experience and to be free to express all of who we are, is why I believe we are here. So yes, the intense pain came back; all the noise and awareness of where I was came back. I was soon rushed off to get a C-section. Aly was…released.

I knew she was an integral piece of my journey. Our growth and purpose together was to function as a team.

I'm a single mom. I haven't spoken of Aly's Dad. We lived together, but I knew the relationship would not last. I was embracing my spiritual path and there was a lot of misunderstanding and resistance. I also had to accept that was for purpose or predetermined. I always felt I was to have a child with this man. I honor him for that. In choosing to move on took a lot of courage, it was very difficult. In reflection, I know that if I was honest and approached him earlier, the situation which had manifested that included a Third party, may have not happened. In leaving him, there was pain around that but I knew I would be okay.

I breast fed for two years. I went away on a conference knowing that I was starting to feel resentful around it. I was asking for a release from that process in my life, in Aly's life. When I got home, she latched on. She turned and looked at me saying, "Oh, Mommy, *sour...sour!*" (Laughter). I thanked God, for that was my answer; it was draining me physically.

Within a month, because of the congenital deformity in my hips, I was crippled. I could walk a block with a cane...with two canes, is all I could do. It was like my body just shut down, or in truth was saying, "Now, you have to look at this."

I was searching for a doctor, as I traveled with my work doing courses to upgrade my knowledge in osteopathy. It took me to San Francisco and Philadelphia. I found a couple names of orthopedic doctors that kept coming to me through various people I met.

I continued my exploration for the perfect doctor. After two years of searching I confirmed for myself, Dr. Rorabeck was the one to help me.

A friend of mine who had just come out of a severe car accident had total reconstruction on his hips done by this man. He told me of his story and I knew this is the man who is going to help me. He lived in London, Ontario. I was in Winnipeg.

After a phone call and a few doctors' appointments to get a referral to see him, I was on the plane to meet Dr. Cecil Rorabeck. He took one look at me, my x rays and asked how much medication I was on because on the x rays the joints were so degenerated. I told I had taken no medication but delved into herbal supplementation and treatments of various sorts. He turned to me, remarked on my stamina and shared that quality of life is important. He looked into my eyes and said, "I will perform the operations needed whenever you want to do it. Just call the office, Karen and we will book you in." A dream comes true.

I truly felt at a crossroads. Mixed feelings of excitement and concern, filled my mind and heart. Now I had to come to the choice, the decision of "these hips have been my incredible teachers for thirty-five years, how do I do this? I need to find a place of letting go and learning all that I needed to learn from this experience. When I got to that place, and it took me about 3 or 4 months (laughter), it wasn't an easy decision. That surprised me.

We booked the appointments for the following year, in May and November. I refer to that year as my birthday, it was just beautiful. It's always overwhelming for me to think about it, the physical freedom and the lack of pain. It was like; I received freedom in a new way or a gift of a new life. My daughter reflected that in the way she walked. To see her Mommy run wasn't an event that ever happened. Oh, it was just totally amazing, absolutely amazing. When I started to feel stronger, I had decided I would leave Winnipeg because I knew I needed to be around spiritual family.

My parents were a blessing in the process as they became a mother and father for Aly. I allowed myself to surrender and realized I needed to reach out and ask for help rather than feeling I had to do it all alone. I believe many of us need to release that thought that keeps us in limitation around the concept of receiving. It was magical to receive. The more I opened my heart to it, the easier it became.

My connection with Doctor Steven Aung was very profound, and the people I met through his work. That drew me here to live. My work with him in Chi Gong helped change my life. It is practiced in the hospitals in China, it is known as Chinese medical breathing. That brought me more physical freedom and added to the growth of my spiritual understanding in my life. I moved out here in trust that everything would fall into place, and it did.

The first week I got here this office was made available; a place for me to work in Calgary was made open to me as well. I felt very supported.

In 2000 after 4 years of no pain and a lot of spiritual growth I decided that I would allow my physical body to soar (laughter), so I went to ski school in Silver Star at the beginning of the New Year and I fell, no one told me how to get off the chair lift! So I found myself going *up* the mountain and realized, "I've got to get off this thing or I'll be going up the mountain!" So I actually jumped off at 4 feet height and broke the glue in my hips.

B: Oh, no…

K: I walked around on them for five months not knowing what was wrong. It was such an unusual pain, nothing like I had experienced. I realized my internal canes were not supporting me.

I happened to meet an avatar, Narayani Amma from India, who is the first incarnation of the Divine Mother of the Universe. Her website is www.narayanipeedam.org. I had first met Amma in 1998 when she/he first came to Canada. I recognized the energy. This was the energy that came to me when I sprained my ankle. I could send this energy into my leg and the pain would go.

I learned how to transform the pain. Pain was an illusion in my body. I could focus the healing energies. That is how studying Chi Gong with Dr. Steven Aung, has helped me. I like to teach people. It is a way of empowering them by giving them the tools to help in their healing on a daily basis.

Statue of Narayani manifested by Amma

When I met Narayani Amma in 2000, I could only ask for help on the second visit. It took me to the second meeting because on the first visit, I didn't feel worthy. I couldn't express my pain, though Amma could see it. I struggled with it all night then I drove back into Calgary the second day and promised I would not leave until I saw her again.

When I opened up and shared this with my cousin, who hosted her at the time, I wept. I needed to acknowledge that I was worthy and knew my life would never be the same if I went home.

The lesson was also in forgiving me for the choice I had made in skiing. I acknowledged also the great joy I had cruising down the mountain with my friend at the time knowing it would be my last. Presently, I live in the mountains. The natives have a saying, why do they walk all over the grandfathers and grandmothers. I choose to enjoy their beauty and strength from the ground.

Amma at Peedam, Bangelore, India

My second visit, as I shared my pain, I simply asked for help. The tears came again. Amma manifested something in her hand which was an amulet of silver. It was of Durga, which is the Goddess of power and wisdom. Within days, I'd sent my x-rays to my surgeon and I was in the hospital in London within two weeks. I knew she was with me.

In this meeting, this energy in a physical form of man was confusing. This was the first incarnation from what I understood on the planet Earth to be the Divine Mother energy. I confirmed it with Lyn who is a friend of mine that is a very gifted medium. Her guide, Jay Paul bows every time I mention her. I knew her being here is very important for the healing of the Earth, as well as for each of us.

With regards to that meeting, it was manifested within days of getting help. My surgeries started again in May and November of the year 2000.

The amulet I had was interesting. We talk of Colloidal silver having healing properties of an anti-viral and anti-bacterial nature. As I went into surgery, I had given this amulet to a friend that had accompanied me to London, Ontario. When I awoke from the morphine and gained consciousness my friend had given me the amulet and I wore it for a day. The next day it had turned a rosy pink. I realized what my body had done. It absorbed the silver from the amulet for the healing properties. It was just phenomenal. I wore that amulet a while but I also discovered I was finished with it. It had served its purpose and actually just disappeared from my sight, to be quiet honest.

B: You didn't give it away...

K: No, it just kind of...left. I was also gifted when my same cousin I spoke of, went to India to visit Narayani Amma, she said, "You give Karen this shawl, it will cover her and hold her in loving energy". I was told to drape it over the end of my bed and it is still there. Being a single mother for the last seven years, I know it's been just a piece that has helped me in trying times, to feel supported. I wrap it around myself and can feel that same loving energy as I do in meditation.

On my journey after I had a C-section in 1993, then my hip surgeries in 1996 and again in 2000, I noticed after my last hip surgery a lump in my left thyroid appeared. It wasn't big, so I never thought about it again until 2004.

B: Mmm...

K: In reflection, I'm saying to myself this is the twelfth major surgery I've had. I found that within myself, just allowing myself to be there, I find peace at being present in the hospital. Releasing the fear, I was doing a lot just by helping other people in that same place. There's such fear being physically in a hospital and I have found that will attract fear and dysfunction.

I found that after the second round of operations in 2000 I was up walking and moving in a miraculous period of time.

My blood levels and my iron were up in three days. I just asked the nurses to leave me to manifest the re-balancing on my own. I was able to physically shift those kinds of things within my structure that gave a tangible result. I felt that I was moving through the experience positively and my Spirit was joyful.

That's what we're looking for, right? That's what we need as humanity.

Lyn had come into my life a few years ago. She is a sister to me. I have previously referred to her. The left lobe of the thyroid, I recently referred to, in 2003 kept getting bigger and bigger. Though I was doing my spiritual work and my energy work around it, it wasn't helping. Well, *I* thought it was getting smaller. My doctor agreed, and after an ultrasound, it had actually grown a centimeter bigger in all dimensions. Oops!

It was really clear to me that I wasn't supposed to fight this. I was supposed to go back into the arena and experience yet again another place of surrender…that I was a spiritual being having a physical experience. My operation was in September of 2004. Lyn was present with me and another very good friend. She was able to help me shift a lot of the energies around some of the surgery and neurological stuff that happened in the operation.

I was in a very extreme position during the operation. I discovered I was thrown out of my body. I was suspended by a long silver cord, and it wasn't time yet for me to go. It was only the start of my journey of the work I have come here to do. I was back in my physical being to wake-up.

B: Do you consider that in the same category of experience as what you described as a near death experience?

K: No. You know what, that experience was very different. That experience was one of remembering, when Lyn put her hands on my lungs and heart, instantly I was thrown out of my body. It was more of a sense of looking down at the operation. It wasn't the same as being in that place of love and compassion.

B: Of being met...

K: I didn't feel anything. I was just suspended. It was almost like I came to this place of well, you know if I got to...if it's time, let's go (laughter). And it was one of indifference, really. It's like, what's happening here? A curiosity. What I came to understand was, the anesthetic, or whatever they used, I responded that way. My system's so sensitive; it actually just threw me out of my physical body. It was that abrupt. I couldn't take it.

It was interesting because Jay Paul, Lyn's spiritual guide came in and said, "You know what you experienced was right, I just want to tell you. That was part of your learning curve in a different way" When you are in an automobile accident or anything like that, we get (clap) thrown out of our bodies. It's the same thing we're kind of looking down going "Hey, what is that? Where am I? Am I really out? Wait a second..." (Laughter). You don't feel any diff... you're indifferent. It's like, there's no feeling. There's absolutely, no feeling, but it's not the same, I believe as in that first experience where I was crossing over where I was getting met by my loved ones. If that's the way it was going to go, I need to find acceptance.

Previous to my thyroid surgery, I went to Maui and had a 33 day retreat. I wasn't aware of the amount of time until I checked the calendar and counted, "It's 33 days!" Many items I bought were 33 dollars (laughter), 33 this or 33 that. And I'm going ok, ok, ok....I get it! I get it!

I kept a journal. That's another book that I'm working on is that spiritual journey. Giving people a guide, so they can actually go there and experience where I was, the animals, the mammals, the turtles and all the beauty of nature in that specific area. If they wanted to, they could use it as a guide to explore for themselves in reaching their potential in that way. I also have come to that understanding that anywhere we are drawn to go on this Earth, we should try and honor that need, for there is purpose in it. In this book, I hope to give people the tools to be present and mindful to the sacred journey they are on by using mine as an example.

I really believe in my heart now the physical journey for me is over...of physical pain.

I said jokingly to a client, nine lives (laughter)...it's like I and a cat, I've had them all, right? (Laughter)

To this day, I still very much am present with Mother Mary, the Divine Mother energies and the angelic realm. Dr. Doreen Virtue, who's a psychologist does work referred to as "Angel Therapy", I resonate totally with that. I also resonate with the Buddhist philosophy. Thich Nhat Hanh's breathing work really speaks to me.

I would rather live aware with my senses turned on 24/7 than it just be something I do one day a week or go to church and only then participate in prayer. It's really become a way of life for me. I think that is what I'm here to share and help people with.

I speak from a platform now of an understanding and awareness. Going through those thirty, or forty-four years, and that's another master number, the physical limitation and trials, if I didn't have prayer, or if I didn't have awareness or sensitivity to something beyond my physical, then I probably wouldn't be here. In that sense many, many times I've been in that dark hole where I've wanted to check out.

B: Mm-hmm. When you speak about guides, angels and the spiritual realm…stop me if I'm using language that doesn't fit for you…

K: No…no…

B: It sounds like that constant relationship, that awareness is a relationship that is collaborative….

K: Well, yes. It's not a separation, there's no separation.

What I've come to learn is, at first, I thought it was separate. I think because my mind needed to manifest that. You know, I've never sat on my bed where I've seen an angel in front of me, but I've felt the loving energy and I don't think I need to see the physical form because I just feel it.

I have a plant in my room by my bed, a spider plant; you know that they have many, many, many, many leaves. *One* leaf will start vibrating…just wiggling….until I notice it, pay attention to it, and ask it what it means, then it will stop almost immediately. Spider plants are about protection. They are about helping absorb and balance the negative energies, the denser energies, or the harder, and more difficult energies. Sometimes it's just a warning, to protect myself or to surround myself with more violet or white light for protection.

I think as our lights grow brighter the denser energies as attracted to it. Like the analogy of moths to a flame. Amma would tell a story of how the beautiful candle lights up a dark room, but the darkness is right there beside the candle. I've had many experiences with denser energies.

One brief experience that was the most empowering and profound for me was, I remember sitting in my room at night with large winds in the valley. The door swings open and I am *feeling* this terror. I stand up and feel this light move through me, out of my heart to this energy. My door closes, the front door closes, the outside door closes and it's gone. I'm feeling, "oh my God, what just happened?" In my life, I have had a journey with those energies. It's not a place I would wish upon anybody. It was part of my life and it's *done* (laughter). I know they love to create drama.

I have chosen to be in this place now of holding this space for light, for growth and for healing.

In response to your question, it is about unity. It's about communion. As a spiritual being, I feel them as part of who I am...and I think more and more with meditation, or Buddhism when I'm with the Dalai Lama, or reading one of his books. I feel I'm with him. Or when I am with Thich Nhat Hanh doing breathing this morning I see, his voice is present, his energy is present. I feel in communion with him...as we do with our animals. We hold our kitten, you know? Or our cat, we just allow our energies to blend and there's this beautiful sense of love and compassion— *unconditional*. It's euphoric...it's heaven on Earth is what it is. I believe that it's manifested here if we choose to open that door.

I believe it's a journey about out heart to *listen* so we can open our mind to *receive*, rather than be so judgmental and mental in our physical limitations about things. That's what I feel as I work. I'll feel an energy come into the room that will help serve in healing, in the healing process, or with me. It will be like; something that comes in, but then also becomes part of my energy. There's an inner dialogue that's created, or inner guidance. It's more of a unity and communion than separation because in Spirit separation is non existent.

Separation is a man-made concept because we're in physical form, we are separate. We are man and woman. I believe, what I've been shown is in the divine order of things there is divine male and female, divine father and mother. They are all in a sense one. I think I just hold that energy and know that others will. It'll just plant the seed of love and understanding. They can choose to water it and nurture it or just let it go for another time.

I truly see my family, my biological family as a learning platform for me. I don't have a strong connection with my family because I was solitude and separate, being in a crib, being in a hospital without touch for a period of time. It is all perspective, for a new born baby it may seem like an eternity, a being who's been inside her mother for nine months.

That's ok with me because what I've journeyed and found was more of a spiritual humanity, a global family. Oh yes and that may include some family members or those that come into my life like yourself or Lyn, or my clients that come through the door, I honor that as part of that connection. Usually it's on that depth, that they do come in. Where I get guided to go, be it grocery shopping and I know I have to run into somebody there and I do (laughter).

I truly believe in all of those pieces. For example, Lyn is coming into town and we're doing our course together. Yesterday, I ran into four different people that are interested in our courses. With that, I know it's time. I am in that conscious awareness about being in the present moment, I take everything in. In that way, I have the understanding, that these are people that are coming forward searching for help. I truly believe that through my trauma and life experience, that is how events unfold.

The surgeons that have done my work for me are people that I have found. With love, I call them my knights in shining armor. Dr. Rorabeck felt like a soul mate to me that was here to help me. His love and compassion was unbelievable. When I hurt my legs and broke them the second time around, his response was, "I'm so...I'm so happy you allowed yourself to have that experience, without judgment on his part. All his students, the young bucks that are still learning reprimanded me saying, "You shouldn't have done that".

London University Hospital, London Ont. Canada,

Dr. Cecil Rorabeck was the only one who embraced me with that divine loving father energy and said, "You know, I'm glad you went for it and experienced the flight of skiing."

My throat surgeon, he was an artist as well. When he came in the morning of my surgery, the first thing he said to me was, "So, are you going to play with me today?" and I said, "Absolutely!" (Laughter) His tenderness, his love and compassion, in that brief moment, though I may never see him again, was moving.

I just trust that he was placed here to help me, and be part of my journey to release this physical piece. It's been profound for me, the support I have received.

B: I'm very intrigued by that support from the medical community, partly because it sounds like part of your process has been about inviting the right people to be in your life at the right time and yet so many people that I speak to have had experiences with the medical community that have really...where they have described feeling that there wasn't an openness to their spiritual self, to prayer as part of their healing.

K: Discernment has been a big piece for me in my life. It's only been in this forty-forth year of my life that I've chosen to write. I've always written. Now it's time to come out of the closet and share it because there are people that need that voice. I think the truth is the truth, no matter whether you are a Christian or Buddhist. It resonates in the heart and you understand it.

When I meet these people, when I journey and I connect, it's an intention and a prayer that I put out in manifesting. I really believe that if I have any bit of fear around my manifesting, it's going to manifest with that energy of fear. I will get someone that's not responsive. And I have. I've gotten some physicians who were not serving for me.

(Laughter) In the beginning, I encountered some real dorks, if I may say, and dentists that have been butchers. I think it's because I had fear. I was just being honest with myself...if I'm going to manifest something, I've got to be able to be in such an open place to receive and trust the Universe in bringing me the right person. If I have any judgment around it, fear, or resistant energy, it will attract that energy.

In our groups, where Lyn and I do the facilitating and teaching, it's about first clearing that resistant energy and being so honest with you. If you are in self-denial around it you're going to create that, you're going to attract that.

I believe for me finding Cecil and also finding Andrew, and having a doctor here in town, that says, "What do you need Karen?" "I need this, can we do that?" "Sure". With me making a brief stop into her office, she'll totally trust what I feel I need. I know that comes with my trust in her and she's reflecting that back to me. I really believe Andrew was reflecting my peace or my openness to receive.

Once I clear those resistant energies and then I ask the angels or guides to help me open myself more to that love and receptivity. Very often, we've been programmed through our evolution, not to receive. How many of us feel we have to do, do, do, and *not* receive? We are not in a loving or worthy enough place within ourselves.

That is the personal journey and the kind of work that needs to happen. I really worked very purposefully before '96 in my first set of surgeries, to clear the lessons.

I went out to Salt Spring Island. I trained with a dance instructor who understood Chi Gong and had trained in the martial arts and Tibetan sound healing. I've done sound healing; I've explored working with charkas. I've done extractions. I've seen monsters come out of my belly from surgeries. My body has been a laboratory. I've allowed myself to journey and be an explorer. I've worked hard at clearing any of those fears or lessons before '96; I feel I did what was available to be cleared by doing these series of things. If anything, I learned and experienced.

My Mom has a prayer group that prays for me. If that's what she feels she needs to do for me, that's great...I receive it! They are in Winnipeg.

B: Traditional, Catholic...

K: Yes, she used to visit those that were dying in the hospital.

When I hold that space of energy of prayer for someone, it's surrounding them with that love and compassion because it's their journey, whether it is to die of their cancer, or in an accident. I have a couple of clients now that are fighting for their lives and I hold them in that place of love and compassion. I ask that their journey be supported with ease and grace. If their journey is about checking out right now, then let it be in that peaceful place. If it's about surviving through it and teaching others, so be it. The loved ones around them, the husbands and children come to a place of learning, love and compassion.

The Dalai Lama talks a lot about compassionate medicine. I've truly come to believe and to know that for most of my clients that are either going through surgery, hopefully this one woman as we speak is, they're in a place of openness and receptivity around it. Then all will go well.

They have found in the osteopathic work, that scar tissue responds emotionally. If you are emotionally at peace with your surgery, the brain, the body has no reason to build more of a barrier. I have next to no scar tissue on my many…and you know if I was to stand naked here you'd see slashes and dashes, such mutilation in my body, from a certain perspective.

From my perspective, they are beautiful and I have next to no scar tissue inhibiting function and structure in my body. I believe, I am and was at that place of peace around the surgeries so that my brain isn't holding the thought "I don't want that surgery. I hate that person, I hate that feeling, I'm resentful to the Universe because of that," such strong feelings.

Women with C-sections that get hysterectomies have huge amounts of scar tissue because they're not at peace, in that place with the surgery. That experience that they've created. It attracts the energy of negativity and the brain goes "Ok, I've got to protect myself even further because I've been cut". So it creates walls and walls of thickness, so that no one can cut you there again.

I work specifically with the brain and the nervous system in my work now with a French Osteopath, Dr. Jean Pierre Barral who lives in Grenoble and teaches at the osteopathic college in St.Etiennes, France. He has taught me about the physical and the emotional aspect of the brains response to trauma. I'm pretty open with clients in asking them, "Do you pray? Do you have any kind of spirituality or beliefs?"

B: You actually ask your clients…

K: Oh, I do! If they're open, I ask that they surround themselves, as I work, with violet light, or gold. They will say "oh, I see really lots of gold light easily."

I will support them by responding," Beautiful, just surround yourself with that on the inside, also in your veins and in your cells".

It empowers them with something they can do on a daily basis. The same exercise regarding the breath. Oxygen is a life source.

The more I am open in discussing it in my life, my clients will say, "Oh, you know what, my Dad just died last week". I feel his energy in the room. I know they need to talk about it. Please be courageous and give them permission to express. For that is a form of healing. The white light or whatever tools that they can accept to work with their grief, dysfunction or pain, be it emotional or physical, support them.

I don't believe the body, the brain, differentiates from physical or psychological pain. You know when we receive news of a loved one dying, we feel sick, and we puke. That's physical. I can touch the puke (laughter), I can smell it, it's not very good (laughter)…and we can get the same response from being hit by a car. Sometimes it's easier for the physical body to heal a physical wound than it is an emotional wound…because it's deeper; its root is in the nervous system.

B: When you pray, what does that look like for you? Is there ritual around that, are there symbols, beads, candles, alters?

K: I create a sacred space which is important. My home is my sacred space. I have a Buddha in my living room; I have a Buddha here in my office. I have a Mother Mary picture there; I have a dolphin on my personal alter with my tinshaws. They make a beautiful sound. I use sound more and more now for clearing space after each patient, for clearing my energy to bring me into a sense of single-mindedness, a focus, a connection when I'm feeling unclear. Candles are peaceful. I have flowers that bloom in my house all the time. My whole home is my altar. Incense as well. These are all forms that I've found the spiritual energies anchor into. A flower, they can anchor into the light of the candle, to the incense for the purification aspect of it.

Essential oils are important to me in the healing process. I use them because it's like white light. It's the purity of the flower. Its oxygenation, I use it between clients and on my hands when I work, over my heart, just to keep me balanced. They are wonderful for the medicinal properties of healing viral and bacterial infection.

I truly believe everything is on the Earth to heal us. In my home and in my office I have chosen to create a sacred space. Everything that's in here has been gifted to me…the salt candle, the bell, the wolf who is a protector, this Buddha here is a gift, the picture is a gift, and this angel is an amazing gift.

When I was in France studying, the office next door burnt to the ground on the inside. This is my shared wall. I had *no* damage (pointing to angel painting on wall). When I came in I just blessed the magnificence. This was created by a client in Winnipeg before I left. I gave her a photo of these angels and I said "Can you paint me a little copy of this, Raphael's angels?" Before I was about to move from Winnipeg, she said, "I have this painting. Remember you asked me to do a painting?"

She worked for the post-office and I knew she needed to do something creative, I knew she loved to paint. I gave her a project just so her heart could express itself. She was very much connected with Mother Mary energy. She said, "Oh, I'll bring it over, but I need my boyfriend's help". When she arrived I said, "That is beautiful!" She carried this huge picture that was three feet by three feet. She shared that she fell in love with the painting and made me a print. This is the print of her original work, she made only one.

B: It's beautiful.

K: When that fire happened and there was no damage in this office, it was also an affirmation for me that, yes, I'm in the right place. There are energies that are beyond my comprehension. I'm trying to open up to understand (laughter,) with what I'm blessed with. We are all blessed with, if we tap into it.

B: It's very compelling...

K: I've been broken into a couple of times with nothing taken. The Police came in and after observing what took place said "this is a miracle, normally this is not a thief's behavior". My CD, Sony Walkman is still here, and a couple drawers were open, but nothing was taken. This is Amma, the Divine Mother, the avatar, the man sitting on the elephant, (Pointing to photograph), .Narayani, who has come to Calgary.

When she first came to Canada in '98 I had an airline pilot who was a client, a woman, and I said, if I'm meant to go and be with her I will. I felt drawn to mention it to her. She offered and I accepted a free ticket for me and my daughter to fly to Toronto to meet with her. I knew it was for purpose. Her palm of her hand is up blessing you. Every time I look at it as I work I *feel* the energy from her...

B: You know, it took me a while to figure out which one you're talking about...because you're saying "her", and I'm seeing a man...

K: Yes I know. That's a gift, the rose quartz...most things have been gifted to me in this room. I've opened myself to receive. I believe this room is made up of those who have come here for healing.

B: I love the picture on your door.

K: Yes, my daughter drew that when we first came here. She was five or six. It is an angel/fairy. As you can see, it is a sacred space. I just see it as a platform of that expression. It's not something that sits in the corner of my house; it's very much a part of the room.

I treat my work table as that as well. I have sage in my drawer. Very often if I need to use it I will. I don't tend to get caught up in using the physical things like that as much in my office. If I need to use the sage with someone that comes in, I'll burn a little bit, if they're open to that, if that's part of their need or experience. A lot of people aren't open to it. I trust if they're here and they don't know why, the work still happens. I just trust that and they trust it because they came through the door.

B: I've asked people how they describe prayer for their own life, or their own purposes…

K: I have a ritual…I wake up, I invoke my higher self, my guide who is a Native American that I've had many lifetimes with. The energies I identify with, I ask him to bless my day, to be with me. If I'm feeling foggy or need anything, then I'll ask for that. I open my heart to all the gifts, the beauteous and bounteous gifts that the Universe has for me so that they can flow through me into the physical world, be it for you, me, or anyone whom I meet. That's a ritual that I do in the morning, I like to do my breathing, my Chi Gong and some meditation. By the end of my day, I'll usually lie down for about fifteen or twenty minutes just to balance and clear my energy.

Before I work, I'll clear the table I'll make sure that the room is clear so that it's not residual energy that you're receiving or the next person's getting, especially when there's emotional grief. This is a room where usually in my office is the dumping bin…is what I call it. I transmute and transform the energy, just asking in prayer that it be released.

I do have one client, and now a very good friend of mine who has said, "This is a way of life for you. For me, I'm just starting, so I need to create prayer here and there and…that is discipline." It can be a constant thought process that's happening in my psyche and in my body.

I have a ritual in the morning and if I feel the need to sound the bell, tinshaws, light a candle or incense depending on how much time I have I'll allow myself to expand into that. For me, it takes time and space as well. I want to be able to make time.

I don't start my day in my office until ten, so I can do writing, or I can have enough time and space to watch the sunrise. I try to watch the sunrise every morning. I don't know if you saw it today, but the vibrancy of the pinks today were *so* electric. That's what inspired my sign outside…the pink, with the blue writing…. Oh, every morning these amazing sunrises! I thought I've got to use this! So my walls are a rose color in my office.

In Maui, that was a beautiful event. Because of the culture and tradition which merges with their spirituality, it's a ritual to watch the sunset. The colors, the hues…are so important for our brains, and for our eyes to visualize and experience. In the sunrise, it is the same thing. People are up at six a.m. walking the beach and experiencing the water, being present to all the colors and the insights that it brings to their day…and the blessings that is brings for their day. That's one thing I like to do. I don't start my work day until ten and I have the time and space to be witness to all that. That is part of my prayer.

B: You spoke about your guide, a Native American guide. Would there be times when you would offer a prayer specifically to Buddha, or be asking something specifically to other spiritual.

K: I invoke in the morning Divine Mother energy, Mother Mary, or Christ energy, I'll just acknowledge it. I feel it within me, I feel like I need that for my day. Who knows how my day's going to unfold. Today, I spent a lot of time with Thich Nhat Hanh with Buddha energy, the sunrise and the breathing. That was my morning. All for purpose, to allow that part of me to be centered enough to articulate and allow the flow of what I need to express to you today. I honor that need within myself. In that way, I honor those energies as in Narayani, when I feel her. I'll invoke her. I'll pray to Mother Mary for guidance around my daughter to help me, or the angels to look after her because…I just can't figure her out. (laughter) Her hormones are too crazy for me right now (laughter). Some days are good, some aren't, so the more I let go. I surrender. I realize we're all spiritual beings having this physical experience. She's got her own spiritual team helping her. She doesn't identify with some of the energies I mention to her.

She retorts, "Oh, Mommy, you try too hard!", and she's *right*. She's absolutely right because we come from that discipline of Catholicism, or *I* do, where we've got to be on our knees, in the church. Now I know in my heart it is not like that for me. My Dad now says, "My church is the outdoors. This is where I am, this is how I pray." He is an ordained minister. I've witnessed his journey.

For my daughter, I have to honor the fact that she sends love to the Earth...it might be two seconds, but it's love in that way, and that's ok. It doesn't have to take you half an hour. It is not the time it is the intention. I might sit ten minutes and go "well, you know what, this is good." (Laughter) The intention was authentic.

We put so many limitations and judgments on ourselves...if it's not done this way, it's not good enough, and I think the fact that we just honor it, is wonderful. I may say, "Oh, Divine Mother, Mother Mary, I can feel you. Be with me today."

B: And also honoring individual differences in what that looks like, what that communication, those relationships look like...

K: Well, like in surgery for instance, I bless everything. I bless everybody and I actually made it a point after my first...second surgery, to look everybody in the eye. They wanted to put me under; I said, "No, not yet." I wanted to look at them and say, "Good morning", so they knew that I was a human being. I could connect with their soul and who they are and bless them. Bless the tools, bless the drills, and bless everything in this room. Cecil walks in and goes, "Why isn't she asleep?" (Laughter) "Well, I wanted to see your beautiful blue eyes and say good morning to you". It shifts the whole process. I believe it does.

I think if more people honored the process that they're in it as a team together; it's not something that someone is doing to you. You are a co-creator in this experience. Bless it and bless everybody, and you know what, I bet you ten to one that everything would go "tickety-boo". It's only within the last ten years. I can speak from that platform that I bless this, bless that. Bless the road that gets me to Calgary, that I'm home safe. Bless that person, who is driving like an old man (laughter), I bless him too, because *I* need protection! (Laughter) I also wish him well for a safe journey. I am calling in this divine energy that's bringing the awareness to a higher perspective.

That's part of my ritual during the day. If things aren't going well, if things aren't in synch or in harmony for me, I'll take that as a sign, "Oh, maybe I'm not supposed to be here". If I can't get onto that website, I probably shouldn't be reading that stuff, or it's not time to do that. The divine timing aspect that the time will be right… "Ah, it's time to do that now. I've gotten through, everything's happening. Whoa, it's taken me five minutes"…rather than struggling for an hour and a half and getting frustrated because I can't create it…it's not time yet. It's like being in the present moment and realizing, "Ok, that's not going to work right now", and accepting it. That becomes a way of life, to start working in that way. You need to put a few minutes aside every day to just make that part of your prayer, your psyche.

B: Are there things for you that you would describe as obstacles in that?

K: It's funny, you know, Thich Nhat Hanh this morning said "hope can be an obstacle, a limitation because you're looking into the future, rather than being in the present moment". Jay Paul has also referred to the concept of hope as not being 100%. I really don't hope for anything. I ask for it and I see it now. I see myself as healed. I see myself as balanced. If I see myself as, "Oh, I've got a bad stomach. Oh, bad stomach. Bad colon, bad colon"…well, what am I saying (laughter)? What energy am I asking to come in? When I work with my clients I see everyone as healed. It's something that is innate. I just hold it in my heart for them. In that way, hoping is saying that you don't have it yet. Deepak Chopra said that in amazing ways, like the affirmation, "I am peace".

In writing my book, "Spiritual Stretches", it's about affirming, "I am". I am peace, I am love, I am beauty, I am worthy, I am Narayani, I am Jesus, I am , I am the mountain, I am that beautiful sunrise. You know what? I didn't believe it for the first while in saying it, but the more and more I said it to myself as an affirmation, the more I realized it brought in the energy, the vibration of peace, the frequency of peace into the present moment in my body. I am love, I am harmony and it's like, oh wow, I can really feel that in my being bringing that energy into my body and it's physical.

They've now done S.P.E.C.T. tests where they can monitor how circulation changes. These are tests that look at the flow of fluids into the brain. The work that Buddhism and the Dalai Lama are doing with the Quantum Physicists regarding meditation and its affect on the brain and the nervous system is fascinating to me.

Bringing in the light, those higher energies, to open up the contraction that is created out of fear and resentment, is one way I work with people. The areas that are holding patterns are those areas of disease. The light, the energy and the oxygen isn't getting into. That's why Chi Gong really opened up a door of that knowing for me because physically I can move and release pain from my body. I know it's an illusion. Pain is something that I'm creating. We all have the knowing to do that for ourselves, so I try to teach those who are open to receive it.

With regards to obstacles, I think what we do is look into the future or we live in the past. I think the present moment is created from the past, and the future manifests itself in this present moment. Whatever this interview will bring... bring for you and for me...and for whoever it reaches and touches, that's my prayer. My own understanding and my reason for putting the energy into being with you is that I truly believe energy is never wasted. The energy will touch one seed, or ignite that seed of growth in someone and that's what it's about because that's where we start to heal.

I truly believe that in healing myself I heal the Earth because we're microcosms on the Earth. We feel the earthquake, when we're in tune that way. We feel disharmony in the Earth and sadness. I don't know if you felt that *overwhelming* grief or fear come from the Tsunami that traveled around the Earth. What I chose to do was breathe it in, process, transform and acknowledge it so that it can move into joy and light. For two days, I was feeling terrified and I didn't know why. Of course, it was that wave of destruction that comes as it hits the land. It went around the Earth and the grief of everybody's energy moving around the planet was also cleansing the planet. Part of that's the expression of the Earth, the grief, the pollution and the abuse that it's taken on that level. To be aware in that moment and say, "Ok, that's done, I don't feel that any more" (laughter). I feel the joy and celebration of it now, transformed." That feels like relief in my body.

There are those of us that are in that place of awareness that are here to help with those processes. I think its important being in the present moment. The obstacles are living in the past of "would a, could a, should a", and going into the future, "I hope I'll create that" and just being present and saying, you know what, I'm going to right now go in that place of forgiveness for myself, for my mother...just release it. Smile to them and know that they're smiling back at you, letting go in that moment. Other obstacles, it would be anchoring ourselves in either of those realities and the obstacle of resistant energy because it really only attracts more fear and resentment. It's a "catch 22", it doesn't serve me…in my life I've learned that. It just attracts crap…like a big magnet (laughter).

(Turning tape over)

B: So you were saying…

K: I do have a prayer shawl it's a gift from India, from Narayani. I will wear it around the house or if I need comfort. I referred to how I received it earlier. I used to bring it to my operations, to the hospital (laughter) or on my drive into Calgary, in a snow storm or when I felt insecure. I used it that until I realized I didn't need it so habitually any more. Now it lies over my bed, and I will, I'll clothe myself in it sometime. The awareness was the strength lives in me.

B: How would you describe your prayer life and the meaning that it brings to your life?

K: I see my life as one big prayer. It started when I was a little girl going into church, just sort of sitting and kneeling and looking at the lights. Knowing there was angels up there, I can feel them, it felt good.

Very often before my surgeries I would go into a cathedral. I stayed at the nunnery at the University of London, Ontario. I would sit in chapel with the nuns. It was a very sacred time for me. I stayed on the floor…on the fourth floor, where people were waiting for heart and lung transplants. I wrote an article on my experience there, with a person passing. The waiting, the trusting and being present in that place with them, I found peace. I find this a place of sacredness.

In Mexico, I went into the chapel and sat. I'll usually go into most chapels. In Maui, I sat in the old chapel in Lahaina. The time usually will be unknowingly three minutes after three or three thirty three or something like that (laughter). For me, it's just a calling to connect in that way. I always find that I make time to do that. I honor that part, even though I don't go to mass. I used to; I knew all that was a beginning for me. The seeds were planted and watered when I was little. Communion, first communion...the whole little bride experience, the white veil...that beauty or that simplicity as well. In that way, I did come from that place of ritual, definitely. Now I feel more with conscious awareness, I make it more my life. My life is more like a prayer...a walking prayer.

B: I'm thinking again of what you said earlier about no separation

K: Yes.

B: Is there anything that you wish we had talked about that we didn't? And as I say that I'm thinking, wishing is very future oriented! (Laughter)

K: I just trust, with the energy that's here right now, I believe everything that has come forth for me to say, has been said. My prayer would be that it reaches those that are willing to hear with love and compassion, for the highest good of all. Let the seeds of positive affirmation, happiness, joy, and freedom be nurtured. It is with intention that we water them and they grow. It doesn't happen naturally. It is a chosen effort.

It is also an effort that one chooses the need to stop watering...causing a cessation or a stopping of the watering and nurturing of the negative seeds. That's ok, because it brings more freedom...but it does take an effort. This didn't come all so naturally to me. I've spent forty four years

71

working through this. I knew at twenty two, I just knew…and I think I said it to myself, I need to find peace. I'm on the path to find some inner peace because I don't have it right now.

It does take an effort. Once you incorporate it into your life, it becomes like washing your face in the morning or brushing your teeth, it becomes involuntary. It just becomes a part of who you are. I hold that space for those who will give themselves permission to put the effort into it, to make that choice. I think that's the place we're at with the Earth as well….so, yes….I'm done! (Laughter)

B: Thank you.

(End of interview)

This interview of my life experience is a support to those who are struggling.

The Universe is compassionate and ever present to our needs along this journey. As Jay Paul and Lyn Inglis have played a part in my journey of remembering, I know this will spark or ignite a piece for you.

Spiritual Stretches

Volume Two

Introduction

Welcome my friends,

I trust your work with the first volume, has served you and that is why you are here to continue your awakening. I am full of joy that you are here and ready to move forward.

We will venture out into our original nature to do healing work with the Earth and ourselves. As the healing journey continues within, the Earth also heals herself, we are here to support that by carrying the universal light and enlightening others to that awareness.

I find the amazing part of this journey for me as I go forward, or inward, I too can bring others to that place as a guide. I live at present in the mountains and always refer to the mountain guide community but this gives the profession another meaning.

My cat, Angel is still with me and sits to my right as I begin another journey with you. The evening moon is close to full in January. I bless this time I have to write and allow Spirit to move through me. In reflection of my lifetime, I have written more in this last month than I believe I have in many lifetimes.

Angel is talking and ready to jump into my lap. She seems excited about something. She jumps up, resting on my shoulder like a throw shawl. I referred to in Volume One of the plants in my home that flower. Well, the jasmine so fragrant blesses my experience here near my computer as well as the vibrant pink Christmas cactus. The amaryllis is soon to bloom in my bedroom along with the violets that are deep purple and iridescent pink. Angel is purring as if to say, Welcome again.

A big piece of this volume focuses on intentions, using our frequencies for the healing of humanity and the Earth. Sending the violet and gold frequencies to the Earth from the place of clear light is the first journey I will take you on. This material is under the assumption that you have spent time clearing the resistant energies.

Opening Blessing

Let us invoke our higher selves, our guides and all beings of light who wish to be present, as we open our hearts to journey deeper into our healing within. We know as we do, we do so for the Earth and all sentient beings. We ask the Universe for its love, compassion, protection and direction as we join into unity, for we are truly one. Know that we work always from a place that serves the highest and greatest good of all.

Working from Clear light

Find a quiet place, working with the breath as a key to centering yourself and bringing you into that place of peace.

As the breath travels into the physical body sense the movement deep within you. If feelings come up re cycle the energies exhaling. Now take a deep breath in and exhale three times. Allow yourself to be in the clear light. We all have our own way of getting there. The meditation with Lyn Inglis is a tool to help those who need direction. Once in awhile it is a great experience to go back and do it again as I have had a deepening experience with Jay Paul every time I experience the meditation.

A piece of guidance around this meditation is, if you set an intention before you do it, be it for some physical or emotional healing, I have had some wonderfully moving experiences where I have come out of the meditation balanced and pain free. Allow yourself to be creative. With arms extended keep expanding with "Yes" to all you are.

In the clear light of our original nature, allow yourself to expand into the vastness of beautiful light and colors. Know that you are surrounded by a million suns, feel the magnitude of energy, the connectedness. As you are in that place of peace, allow yourself to travel through the Universe to the mother Earth planet.

Once you see her, send a beautiful violet and gold ray of love and compassion to her to surround her. At this moment, as you sit and experience the connection, know that this energy is coming from your universal heart. At this time, you can allow the planet to come into your universal heart and rest there. This energy is continually running until you choose to disconnect from it. This can be for infinitum or just for this exercise. Take the time to make a choice by letting go of the experience or choosing for it to continue.

Allow your attention to come back to the vastness of your energy and light. Then slowly become conscious of your physical body.

When you come back fully, open you eyes and take a few moments to breathe in purposefully to ground yourself. If you get up and walk you may notice the heaviness you feel in the Third Dimension, in form. Acknowledge that sensation as part of your learning and awareness.

An insight I had as an extension of this exercise, was one day I was walking down into town and looked up at the blue sky. I started to become aware of this violet and gold energy raining down on me. I made the conscious decision to keep the energy running to the Earth planet when I did this exercise. I often can feel the mother planet inside my physical heart which is our universal heart during the day it is a comforting feeling for me. The experience I had that day has become part of my understanding now and it has opened my journey into conscious awareness of my multi Dimensionality here on Earth. We will cover this later on.

I will share a few profound breathing exercises of Thich Nhat Hanh's that can be done anywhere. Breathing in, I am the mountain, breathing out, I am solid. This is done to help stabilize and strengthen our being emotionally and physically.

The next is breathing in, I am a flower, breathing out, and I feel fresh. This is wonderful to rejuvenate and restore the damage done in our body from negative thoughts or experiences. When we are fresh and smelling sweet, we are attractive and alive to ourselves. Therefore we expand into all of who we are with the beauty and grace that is within us. The butterflies of the Earth will dance with us.

Release the need for drama in our lives.

The denser energies, when they are playing out are usually what I call, the Third Dimensional energy. When we come into a clearer place the denser energies that we have been holding for years, in either thought forms or in our physical body, will create chaos. For example, I was working through clearing some thoughts when someone reflected to me some density of thought that was clearly stopping them from moving forward. With love and compassion, I went into my heart to see what they needed to hear.

In changing my thoughts around them I can help them clear. My limitation of thought can create a projection that they can act out in, if they choose to. It is like the term buying into someone else's reality. For example, if my mother believes me to be bad, I may accept that projection and turn around and act out in negative ways.

In Spirit, when we work, the tangibility is non existent for that is not how it manifests itself in Spirit. We have created the human mind, in knowing from reading what is in a book or form or email. The insecurity we have as a species in journeying into our Inner net to receive all the knowledge that is there, we sensor ourselves. There is so much doubt which is Third Dimensional energies or densities stopping us from reaching our potential.

Many people will manifest disease or physical pain out of an expression of these energies. We need to empower and trust in our guidance on a constant basis. As we create the constant flow of that connection it will always serve us.

The heart holds our original nature and the keys to the knowledge and wisdom, we as spiritual beings have as our birth right. Keys can be frequency, color, sacred geometry, and light. I would suggest you start being aware or conscious of opening yourself to receive these keys of awareness in this way. Love is the highest frequency and can heal all things. It can transform the densest of energy. It is to know in our hearts without a doubt that this is the truth. Sounds are also a key. Self-love is the way to open these doors, expand into the vastness of who you truly are.

I am you and you are me, we are all one.

Dawning of a New Day Meditation

This will take you to a place where the Earth will evolve into its Fifth Dimensional frequency. The sun will still be the same sun only you will start to see it with different eyes. How you see, your perspective will begin to change. The insights you have will be clearer and will start to see events that unfold with what their universal purpose is rather than the Third Dimensional drama that they have been holding.

In meditation stance, come into the clear light focusing on the mother Earth planet. It is the dawning of a day. The sun is coming up over the horizon. You notice that there are some places that the sun touches and others are left in the shadows. The sun makes its way over the sky, journey with it. As the sun begins to set and the coolness of the evening arrives, know that it is a time for healing. We can rest in sleep.

It is the dawning of a new day, as the sun rises in the sky there are colors of violet and gold, blue and silver. A celebration of color, reaches out to all who see it. As the sun rises in the sky all is touched by the sun. No area is left untouched by this sun. As it journeys across the sky know that a new day is passing. The spiritual aspect of the sun is showing itself to you. In this reality, there is no need to place your hands on others for they are already healed. There is no need to journey out onto the waters, for the oceans are already healed. There is peace and harmony. Joy and celebration fill the air of this new day.

Breathing in the Beauty

The resonance of beauty is everywhere breathing it in acknowledge the beauty and with deep gratitude see yourself as beauty for it is being reflected to you.

Oh my goodness. Yes, Yes, Yes the whiteness of the snow reflects the white of the light that heals. Breathing in I pull the whiteness into my Third eye holding it in my pituitary gland. I exhale the toxicity I have held there in my brain and nervous system.

The Vase of Impermanence

Last night I watched the Dalai Lama in a learning DVD filmed in Finland. It was the resonance of being in his presence and the frequency he holds which is like the frequency of our original nature. Many sat with their eyes closed absorbing the magnificence of the encounter. I know for me by the second hour I was feeling like I wanted to go to sleep, a feeling I get when I am being pulled out of my body to meditate.

I remarked to my friend, Lyn, the experience of being with him is what it is truly about.

He was talking about impermanence. I suddenly was shown in my mind looking at a vase and seeing the spaces between the molecules and atoms ever changing. I sat with that image embracing the experience and perspective.

As I slept the following night I had an amazing experience. I was light the beautiful clear light the vastness of who we are and like a funnel cloud it was focused on my body. I was the light and not the body I felt the non attachment to my physical self and with that the light came into this body and like a

Universe I could feel and see the vastness of you. I was even in my physical form the Illusion, the space between the cells were vast filled with light. I was then conscious with that same perspective. The non attachment and the clarity of the experience I still am holding with me now. It has brought great peace and freedom. I feel light in my heart and joy, joy, joy.

In sharing this with you I hold the resonance so you to can journey to that place and ask your guides for this awareness.

Rainbow Frost Cloud

This same morning I saw a rainbow in a frost cloud in the air lining the valley. I felt blessed acknowledging it, for this is a way the Universe communicates to me.

Last week Jan 31, 2005 my daughter Aly and I witnessed a wonder. I always felt in doing the meditations and perusing this path of understanding, I felt deep in my heart the day would come, where I would witness a rainbow cloud. I wasn't sure of the significance but it would be a turning point of the Fifth Dimensional experience for me. I wasn't aware totally what it would bring but I had a deep knowing it was a sign for me.

That morning, the clouds were moody and the weather was unseasonably warm. As the sun was rising there was a thin sheet of haze or cloud behind dark moody clouds that were traveling quickly across the sky. As they parted, I could see the sky filled with color, a huge spray of cosmic green alive with celebration. I called for Aly to come and witness this. We then saw more of this wonder as the whole border of this scrim was colored with large sprays of this green and orangey pink. Ten minutes rolled by and we just sat and watched, witnessing the newness of this. As the sun rose the color faded. I was excited like a child at a birthday party.

Painting your Guardian

Aly and I sat in meditation with the paints laid out and paper before us. We ask for the connection to our higher selves and invite our guide or guardian to make themselves known. I open my heart to blend the energies of who we are so you can guide my hand and eyes' creating what represents you in my life. We also lit a candle to set the sacredness of this activity.

Craft activity around Relationship

In the same way, prepare for a sacred activity as Aly and I did previous to this. In this activity we gathered as a group of women with our children. Our intention here was to explore relationship. Harness our intuitive creating skills without censorship, creating our partners to be, guides or ourselves.

I first created out of pipe cleaners, fabric, gems, flowers anything that was there that expressed me, was molded together. To my surprise, in a split second after, I was drawn to create a partner that was on the horizon.

Self Portrait in fabric

This is created with a wooden ring woven with beige crepe fabric. Gold ribbons are tied around top representing the crown, a white flower in the solar plexus, a dried rose, Lace wraps my legs, a rhinestone bracelet, a seashell, blue flat stone for the face all grace the circle representing aspects of me.

The creation you see above you had birch wings and the structure hung from a piece of wood brought from Jericho Beach on Vancouver Island.. The face, I balanced an oval gem stone of deep blue and electric green, possibly azurite, with hawkish feathers in the chest. I wondered if what I had created was my guide Red Hawk. The hair was grayish and long wrapping around his body. His right arm was clocked in gold fabric while the left was a healing green color.

I hung these two creations on my wall for six years when I was single. Recently having moved in with my partner, I have let them go. Sharing them with you as an inspiration is another tool you can use to explore your potential.

Relationships that are toxic

It takes an incredible amount of courage and belief in your truth to release the old patterns of behavior in our lives. Sometimes I ask for extra assistance knowing that I feel vulnerable and need the extra help from my guides or the loving energy of the Universe for this to manifest. In choosing different, we hold the resonance for others to do the same. Blessings to you in this time of change, celebrate this freedom of choice.

Healing within, is healing our relationship with the Earth and others.

As we do this work our surroundings may begin to change. Hopefully they will, for this why we are doing this work. Be gentle with yourselves. As I said in Volume One of Spiritual Stretches, remember our choice of colors we wear will alter, or our home may become more basic, clearing away the clutter that anchors us in an old reality. Celebrate the shift.

Fear will only breed fear.

I am not sure whether you have experienced this dynamic where the energy of fear attracts fear. Be diligent in this practice for clearing of these resistant old patterns is integral in moving forward.

Family dynamics

This setting is always been a major teacher for me. Here in this forum we find our greatest teachers. Embracing this new perspective will start to ease the drama around this platform of experience.

Choosing Truth

Truth, the frequency of that word, as in love or fear has its own resonance. That is why words can be hurtful. They can stab, punch or drill a hole in our consciousness and trigger all sorts of responses from our psyche.

Blessing the experience or word can help change its frequency. Also going into your heart and asking yourself what is the truth. When you discover and the truth speaks to you, hold what is your heart and stay there with the knowing that you are the truth.

Many people will challenge our worth and hit us in our Achilles heel. As I have said, the denser energies are playing out quite dramatically at present. If you have been doing the Clear Light Meditation the image of the triangle is used. Use the tools you have in your toolbox. Go into that place where the clarity and truth of who you are re balances the experience as in the Clear Light Meditation. It is important to feel empowered in these times.

Peace is another frequency or key in keeping in balance and harmony.

Discerning our Truth?

Reflections others hold are of us. Allow yourself to look within first, then around and ask your heart what the truth is.

Ego and mental energy will cloud the truth; the heart holds the truth.

When clients come in and are primarily holding mental energy, it looks like a fuzzy cloud around them. They have a hard time putting sentences together or they question themselves. I will know that I need to clear that energy first because it is influencing the physical state in their bodies. When the energy is cleared, space is created for the healing energies to come into place.

I urge you if you are feeling like this at the end of a day, take those few minutes to lay in meditation, sound the bells to shift the energies or take a salt bath with candles to help you re-balance your energy.

I have personally experienced far too often in my learning curve when the energy of irritation creates arguments or misunderstandings. Hurt feelings result between family members. This energy loves drama. Be compassionate with yourself creating the space to rebalance. It is a true gift to all around you.

Self Portrait

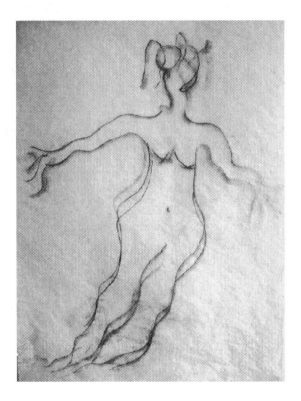

I was attending The Indigo Conference in Ashland, Oregon put on by the Beloved Community with James Twyman, Neale Donald Walsch, fabulous speakers and singers. Aly accompanied me. This was an event we embraced together.

There was a choice of active workshops to participate in. Aly and I started out in this special type of painting with ink, where we used our hands to create. Tissue paper was placed on a hard plastic backing with colored ink, we joyfully began.

I wish I could remember the woman's name that created this form of expression. I understand she has a center where disabled people come for therapy using this creative forum. Aly and I loved it so much we stayed for two sessions.

She talked about allowing the flow in meditation to guide you and your hands from your heart. This resonated with me beautifully. Within seconds, from focusing on my heart and breathing in, I exhaled, my hands moved with the intention of creating a self portrait. I was surprised with what I saw. It moved me to tears.

Having been compensated with hip deformity since I was born, I didn't have feet or legs in the portrait, but ones that appeared to float. The beauty in the head and hair was where I put my focus as an actress for several years in my lifetime. My hands were just energy.

I shared with the instructor that my struggle physically through this life time was a focus of healing for me. In accepting the imperfections and embracing the gifts and awkwardness has been freeing. I know now what I deemed awkward is only perception and shifting how I see my unique beauty.

For more information about James Twyman's internet courses, such as, "Spiritual Peacemakers," and "Reclaiming your Indigo Power," please explore his website at www.emissaryoflight.com. I have completed them all, and have found them to be supportive and life awakening.

Freeing our Pain

Pain is the denser energy expressing itself physically. Free it with this knowing. It has served me until now and I am ready to let it go. Ask it whether it would like to be free and transform into something else, the sun or the waterfall. I did this and with joy I heard its reply. Off it went. Inwardly, I said to the pain that I honored it, for it was created to bring me into this place of knowing, it was here to teach me. Pain can also be Karmic energy. This energy is needed to be rebalanced from a past life experience. We have incarnated with the residue of this energy to rebalance it. That will be discussed further in Volume Three. My awareness was that I needed to release, transmute or balance this from a past lifetime.

Breathing in, I feel my pain in the left jaw, breathing out; I smile to my old friend pain

The Web of Pain

I can see a web that holds the vibration of the energy of pain. If we can see pain manifested in that way, it will alter its perception for us. We have been all things. I am sure I have been pain, the wound, the virus, and bacteria. This is something I am going to have to go deeper into to discover this truth. I know in our hearts we would like to think we have always incarnated in a positive form. I know from my journey of lifetimes that I have been saint and sinner.

Dialogue with our pain

This technique is used quite often now with therapists that acknowledges that the pain, cancer, virus, bacteria or parasite itself has a consciousness. I talk with it as previously mentioned.

Cohabitating with other frequencies

I never realized this until I passed from my physical body a 12 inch long round worm. I was taking Oregano Oil and Cod liver Oil to fight some throat infection my daughter Aly was fighting. As a preventative, I was doing this. Little did I know, I was taking the parasitical dosage. Sunday, I was writhing in pain with severe diarrhea and vomiting. The early hours of the morning left me exhausted.

The next morning, I woke up feeling peaceful. This expansive peace had me where I felt I didn't need to do anything. I got up with the urge to go to the bathroom. I thought "How can I? With nothing left in me from the night before."

After the movement I stood up and turned around drawn to look at what lay before me. I couldn't believe it. There it was. I took chopsticks cleaned it off and placed it in a container. I apologize if this makes you squirmy but my awareness is that the consciousness of the parasite was not within me any longer. I instantly felt that my waist was 3 inches smaller and I was more myself than I have been for awhile.

I know that the denser frequencies can't exist in an environment of a higher frequency. I took that as a sign, I was doing some clearing out of the old ways. Jay Paul talked to me about my health. I needed to stay on a cleansing regime guided by my Naturopathic doctor. I bless her in her insight and humor in helping me transform this experience into a learning one. After going onto www.drnatura.com I learned about parasites, the how, why and what we can do to release them from our system, also the severity of hosting these energies. Releasing them is a process of purification.

I found that it was important to be gentle with myself and not go into self judgment. I needed to see the experience as a gift of learning. That was how I worked through it.

I think we continually process through the aspects of this Third Dimensional experience.

I must admit I went back to my writings and included parasite in the part that covered the manifestation of the denser frequencies, as virus and bacteria.

Healing from our original nature

I ask you to journey into the place of clear light. Here, we are of light and energy therefore releasing the sensation of the physical body. Set the intention to rebalance any pain and all energy systems. In this place, we clear the spiritual, then the emotional, and the physical therefore can rebalance. I find it is a place when I come back that I feel at peace. My stressors and physical pain does dissipate.

Healing with the fabric of the Universe

Journey into the place of clear light and draw from the green, blue and gold threads of the universal fabric to mend any imbalances within yourself. The green frequency is physical healing, the blue is emotionally healing and the gold focuses on the any healing regarding mental energy or the body's innate intelligence.

Healing the unseen and sub conscious energies that manifest our pain. I have shared various techniques in Volume One to deal with the attachment of unseen energies. A Medicine Buddha, Karma Rinpoche once said to me after a ceremony he performed to help me with energies I felt I had acquired in treatments, "remember that all is an illusion."

Healing our wounded perceptions

If we truly have the need to see someone or a situation as a villain we will manifest that reality in our lives, the self fulfilling prophecy.

I had a situation where a family member had a difficult time understanding me and my lifestyle. An opportunity arose in which a Third party shared false information which colored her wounded perception. I received a phone call filled with negative energy, accusations and profanity. I created a boundary around the abusive language and ended the conversation.

Instantly, I felt this bubble of energy around me. A year ago I would have taken it to heart as it pulled me far off my center. I would cry and be unsettled for days. In this energy, I didn't feel anything but compassion and sadness for the choice this person made.

It took over a year of time, space and personal healing for this individual before they came around where they could be in the same space as me, my need to feel safe. This energy primarily rippled through the family unit. It was instantly shown to me who believed in me without condition or proof and what the colors or conditions were around the expectation of favors or generosity. I was shown integrity was in question.

There was expectation in the giving, so frustration was created and anger. In my heart, when I give freely, there are no conditions. It comes from a place of freedom. It flows. That is how I define love in my life.

It is integral how we choose consciously to define love in our lives.

Personally Defining Love

Take this moment to breathe in and fill your sacred heart with the gold and God light of understanding. Now ask to be shown how you define and live love out in your life. If it is not in harmony or alignment with your heart, change it. See where it falls out of place and ask for extra help and guidance in re aligning it to your higher purpose, so you can manifest and be all that you are in this lifetime.

White Swan Hot Springs, B.C with Heart Rock

Working through the illusions

With this previous example, looking deeply I saw someone who was hurting and in a lot of pain. Frustrated in her experience of life and struggling with some deep inner issues on how she defined herself.

I knew in my heart, the truth is the truth. I did nothing out of step with my integrity. The wounded perceptions created misunderstanding. That was sad. It is reflected all over in our world.

When Aly shares personal events at school that emotionally affect her they are founded on wounded perception. I share with her that wars are created out of simple misunderstandings as well. She sighs, a sense of relief knowing clarity is important.

What is real?

Recognizing projections placed on you and releasing them

The projections placed on me as being the villain, manipulative, one who takes advantage of others, was all an illusion. I usually say to Aly when she comes home sad from something someone at school has called her, I ask her to go into her heart to find out what the truth is. Is it true? More often, she will smile and turn to me saying "no." I know it was hurtful what you were accused of and she will say yes. She will sometimes have a good cry. When that energy has settled I will guide her to take a breath in, hold her breath, feel the sunlight fill our bodies with light and love. Does that feel beautiful? Supported? Now as you breathe out, let go of all the awful feeling stuff. She will smile again, go on her way, have a healing bath or a little cry again as the nervous system releases the energy that was projected on to her.

We can have energy projected into our energy field and as long as we acknowledge it as an illusion, we can easily let it go. We can have this same energy projected into our energy field and if we buy into it as reality then we will start to play out in the drama it is working to create. Hard feelings, an argument, name calling, depression sadness and anger, mostly related to ones ego are usually the outcome.

Knowing in your heart what is and isn't yours to process.

Working closely with Jay Paul he has taught me this and I incorporated it in my daily life so I don't pick up on the chaos that is playing out. From this place I can see that it is someone else's process.

I do acknowledge to myself for example, that my sister had hurt feelings therefore has created this agitation and has spoken harshly to me because of her irritation. Seeing and knowing it for what it is, is freeing. I chose not to play out in the unfolding drama by arguing or defending myself. That is ego. I left her alone. Within time and when I am guided to, I will talk to her. When she is more open to hear the truth or see the event that was created by her as her issue.

If we can see our lives as a play upon the stage, the script is already written before we incarnate and the people around us are hired actors. They too, have signed up for these parts before they incarnated. In Spirit, as we all leave the stage we belong to the same company. All are friends even those who have played the villain, lover, mother, murderer and friend.

We have free will to make choices to come from fear or love in our responses to life. I have found that coming from a place of love radiates healing for all around me. In its quiet way, it also in its power helps without words those struggling in these hard times.

Creating space, surrendering and how we do that?

Letting go of the outcome of the situation by stepping out or stepping back literally is like freeing or removing ourselves physically and emotionally from the situation. It allows us to see clearly.

Challenge your inter- net universal information

In meditation, use these three topics to explore what images or information you receive from the deep well of universal knowledge that lies within you.

1) Journeying to other time lines.

2) The spiritual Universe is very different than the physical Universe.

3) The re-wiring of the Fifth Dimensional frequency within ourselves.

Changing our perception of ourselves, in the action of choosing to see differently

Seeing ourselves as the God head, the universal mind, a spiritual being in a physical experience has allowed me to feel free.

Setting an intention for healing and how it can unfold.

I set an intention for healing because I was grinding my teeth at night. Two weeks after, this event occurred. I was surprised how the pieces started coming together.

There has been a lot of dense energy expressing itself over the last few weeks around me. In my friend, Lyn who got so ill after arriving in Canmore to do some profound work with our new groups, the book and her guidance in readings or spiritual counseling sessions. My daughter, Aly then got ill with a stuffy nose and tentative sore throat. Four members of the Monday night group did not attend the second class because they were ill with a various series of expressions of a viral or bacterial invasion.

I myself have been fighting it all along bringing in the clear light merging my energies with spiritual family in the clear light and then coming into my physical form stronger and clearer, also holding the frequency of loving myself as I do this.

I awoke Sunday a.m. with violent diarrhea as mentioned previously. My stomach was heaving and very specific in its pain. The morning came where I managed to vomit accompanied with diarrhea, a total purging. By 3pm I was feeling better. I tentatively ate supper in the form of soup and it was no problem. The next morning as I rose I needed to go to the bathroom. I found that odd because I thought so much came from me the other day that it would be at least two days before a movement. Well, I went and I felt drawn to turn around to see what was in the basin. A 12 inch worm, as I previously mentioned, appeared dead. I awoke feeling very peaceful. I did put an intention out to heal my mind and the grinding of my teeth. I had heard from someone that parasites could be a cause of grinding.

Well, my sleep the night before, I don't think I moved. I remembered waking with a slight clench. In the a.m., I felt empty or spacious on the inside. I stood at my window facing the mountains. I felt at one and at peace. Nothing was moving through my head as to what I needed to do or want. Could it be that the worm consciousness had affected me that much. I did a meditation to the "Eternal Ohm's," a CD soundtrack. The cat, Angel joined me by settling in on my lap. She then sprawled out along me in this twirled stretch she likes to do. I called the hospital and my brother, who seems to be the parasite specialist in our family, but no one was there. I took it as a sign that I needed to go within. I didn't even want to bother my friend, Lyn today, until I moved through this. I placed the dead specimen in a container and will connect with my naturopath tomorrow.

It was all making sense to me the process of elimination from the body.

As I walked, I was drawn to the river. The huge chunks of ice had broken free from what had accumulated there. The river was racing along at a good 6 knots. The rhythm inside of me was a lot slower, I stood on the bank and I was with the several ice chunks some that were 5 feet by 3 feet large ones racing effortlessly surrendering to the flow and speed of where the moment was taking them. That is all that was there. I stood several minutes and was vaguely aware of people passing me. These ice blocks as heavy as they were, were supported by the water suspended as one in the journey. Peace and no resistance, a total acceptance. When the ice collided or bounced off each other it made a beautiful tinkle and continued on its way.

By the time I had arrived home, the energy around the morning event has dissipated. I bless the insights that came from the experience.

I will also mention that I did share the experience with my daughter, Aly, as part of her learning curve. Very often we talk about ways the denser energy can affect us and this gave her some tangible, yet in her mind "gross" proof.

This is incredible. I have heard from another member of our development group who on the weekend had a blocked bowel. Another member had a twisted colon, I passed a parasite, Lyn had been sick, Aly has low grade Mono, our new mother of the development group was unwell; another member, who is a cancer survivor was coming down with something. It is a humbling time, but also a time were I feel I need to ask for extra protection. Put on an armor of light to repel the denser energies that are at huge purpose right now.

In this place of love and compassion, I am spacious on the inside and bewildered. Iran has had a quake and many are freezing and dying from the cold. I had asked Jay Paul about Iran and Iraq being so close. He mentioned their time in the earthly events unfolding was later.

I am blessed with this personal experience. I was asking for healing around grinding my teeth and also the denser frequencies that were at play. I know that when this was all unfolding the waves of energy coming down alongside my body were numerous as a golden shower to help with the release process. I am honored and feel grateful for that help.

I lay on my bed with a rush of energy from head to toe traveling alongside me like a wave. It has created space for the higher frequencies to come in more profoundly and simply. As I look at the mountains here I see them in a new way; peaceful, expansive, but an oneness as in connecting with an old friend every morning.

Reciting the ohm's brings me into the quietness of peace and my cat Angel instantly joins me with the knowing that it is beneficial for both of us. Beautiful music fills our home blessing it and our office; an inward time to hold energy for the Earth and humanity.

The group classes have been wonderful in letting go, creating the space for those involved to heal. Supporting each other, sensing the vastness of energy and love coming from them, for we are one. Watching the light bulbs of excitement, affirmations come to them and see the seeds burst forth into their next stage of growth are beautiful.

As the resistant energies let go, tears fill the eyes of those involved. The group is there to support and nourish without condition.

I sense we have created a safe environment to grow. Now everyone can move forward into the community and hold the space and energy for others to grow as well.

Our next stage of our evolution will be attained by healing within and then extending the energy outwards for those around you generously without condition, our inner evolution.

On an emotional level, I needed resolution around the parasite experience. I had the intention to release it fully with help from the group. I found that when I left, I felt the physical pain gone from where I was holding some self judgment. I needed to perceive it as a celebration of my inner evolution. Throwing away the specimen and thanking it for the learning curve, was difficult for me, but I eventually did it.

With the clear intention of needing extra help from my unseen friends was important for me to acknowledge. Please ask for help. There is abundance waiting for you, if only you ask and open your heart to it.

Healing self judgment or issues around unworthiness, I expand my arms to that beautiful sun and repeat "yes" until I feel that resonance of love enter me and shower every cell of my being. Give thanks and acknowledge the presence, with conscious awareness, how it opens up your journey of inter connectedness and oneness with all things.

I did celebrate with a glass of bubby white wine to complete the 3 D physical event. I expressed its completion in that way.

Painting Your Guide

Allow yourself, in a sacred space, to set the stage at a table and go into meditation. Invoke your guide, and ask that he/she help you create on paper with color what represents your guide, whom you feel present around you.

In painting this picture of Jay Paul, lips often came out very red. I placed the brush in water and kept stroking the paper gently with only water on the brush. After a few minutes passed, a spark of red came out of the paintbrush which created the color of Jay Paul's lips. It happened on another painting I did of him, as well. The mark on his face was a turtle shell that represents wisdom, I am told. His electric green eyes, I have seen in meditation. They initially shocked me. I was not expecting such an electric emerald green.

Have fun and with love, embrace this intimate connection. All these activities draw one closer in celebration of who you are.

The Switchboard of the Universe

In talking with one of the people in the development groups, they needed an explanation as to how I see the universal fabric and how that works for me. As I began to articulate about the colors, that every color or emotion has a unique vibration, so do these elements or qualities we can access in the universal fabric of light. This is who we are. Using it can help enhance the healing of ourselves in this journey.

Lily Tomlin, the actress, was infamous in her character at the operational switchboard, plugging people into various connections. This analogy can be used in drawing on the specific vibration we need for help or inspiration.

As I write, I go into that quiet place where I draw with intention the universal wisdom and knowledge to serve me as I write. It is like I get plugged into that specific channel and the energy flows down my crown and into my body. It has a physical sensation that I recognize. I can now know with my physical being what that feels like and I let the flow come through to the computer.

Such is the same with channeled writing. Allow yourselves to sit in that quiet place and journey up into the clear light. Access that thread and connect yourself into the switchboard. Ask that frequency come down through you. Wait patiently and trust that whatever ideas or images come are for purpose and start to write. When it stops acknowledge that as well, for it is a new learning as to how that energy system flows and works through you, for we all have different gifts.

Embrace the explorer and trust with peace.

If one needs healing, the same analogy can be applied. Plug into the universal switchboard and wait. Breathe in, trusting where you feel guided to place your hands. You may also feel inspired to say a mantra or speak. If the guidance comes that a specific doctor in your community can be of help, trust that. I know, many of the therapists come for treatment when they feel drawn to and I encourage that response, for they are starting to listen with all of who they are.

In painting or any exercise, integrate the universal switchboard and note how it augments or shifts your experience. For me it deepens awareness and takes me to another level of who I am. I giggle when it surprises me.

You are in the driver's seat. How frequently you choose to explore and the effort you put into the experiences is your choice. No one can affect you, but you, I can share and the rest is up to you. I know I am stating the obvious but sometimes it needs to be spoken. Bless you as you choose to create your adventures.

Today as I awoke, the image of the mother Earth planet was toxic, polluted with huge missiles from global devastation, pollution of atomic waste, nuclear waste, garbage, excretion and oil. I saw the planet, in its entirety of waste, on so many levels. I had never encompassed that so clearly before. It saddened me.

This amazing peace came over me and I felt the presence of Red Hawk and Jay Paul. I was being brought back to the time in Earth's history where the beauty and love filled the shores of Lemuria. I could walk towards the ocean and the turtles would come and greet me. Sharing energy on the shoreline, the sun bright with nurturing love and the gentle breeze all are in harmony and peace. I lived on the beach in a grass hut. It was immaculately clean and I celebrated the joy of being on this planet as spiritual beings having a physical experience.

This energy has brought my cat, Angel to me purring. It also attracted my daughter, Aly, who has joined me on the bed, as well. We hold each other breathing and acknowledging the images we are receiving. Giving them voice and talking about it holds the frequency that was brought through us in the present moment. It grounds, the experience for us.

When we go through dense times, we need healing and the transforming of these energies. So does the Earth need to be reminded of the frequency she once was, before this journey of experiencing the denser vibrations began.

Let go of the old need to verify your intention, for your work is in alignment with Spirit. Trust it all will fall into place. Trust and it is so.

The white light of protection is your grace. The spaciousness of Spirit, I embrace in celebration. I have my human mind that has the urge to close in on it. I have asked for additional support in my doubting this expansion, for truly, the Universe is within me. The white dove of peace resonates in my cells ready to take flight, "Is it time to fly yet?" Yes, my love.

As always, when I feel trapped I envision myself in flight with the freedom of space inside and out. Beauty is everywhere, as beauty resides within.

A beautiful movie I have watched many times is "Powder". It makes several references in support of what I have shared. It is a great Aha moment.

Creating Space

The gentle green arched moon image is within me. As I sit back to create space for growth in teaching, many energies are working with me and through me. Enlightening, guiding, loving and I sit back, holding the space for that to happen. Blessings, as snow falling is everywhere in abundance.

The Universe's way of creating opportunity

Marion is a hairstylist, who recently had a treatment with my naturopathic doctor. The morning before seeing Marion, I had a phone call from a woman wanting an appointment with me in my office, I told her that my day was planned and we would have to look at another day. When I went to Marion to get my haircut, in conversation it was revealed, that she was there previous to my treatment with Dr. Herwig. It was also her roommate who wanted an appointment with me. It always titillates me how perfectly the Universe orchestrates my life.

Channeled writing from a development group.

My dear family,

It is with pleasure and love that I come and share with you. The universal consciousness opens with your light for your light is one of the keys you hold to help transform the densities on the mother Earth planet. With joy and effort, be diligent in your practice for as the pebble in the pond ripples the water, so do you on this Earth plane as you hold thoughts of love, peace and beauty. No energy is ever wasted. As you stand in a forest in a part of your world where you live and meditate, hold the energy of gratitude as it ripples from you over the land in all directions.

Many of you have Native American gatekeeper guides. They remind you of your gifts that you shared in that lifetime. In becoming the sum of all your experiences, you draw on all your gifts, for you have been all things. I am with you always. I say, I am made of millions of minds of the universal consciousness. I come into communion with you and say, I am you; you are me we are all one. Open your heart and mind to receive.

Being Open to How energies Communicate

The following are a selection of incidents involving the Intuitive Development Groups that Lyn and I were running. They were learning curves for me on how energies communicated, that have passed over and some signs to look for.

Colin

The morning came on the day we were to all meet at Three Sisters, a mountain village, to sense some energy that was playing out in a neighborhood. It lay across the valley from my condo. When I connected to the area, I sensed a young boy. His image was very clear.

That evening, as I journeyed over to the other side of the valley, the land's energy shifted as I soon approached the area. I closed my energy field down and centered myself because I was feeling vulnerable and wanted to see whether I would still receive, if I consciously closed my energy. We greeted Jack and Karen who lived on this street. They were warm and gentle.

We walked around the block and spent time outside exploring the ravine, the mining road and walking by the homes that had a lot of activity. I sensed presences on the balcony, and the homes that had the energy playing out their aura was different. Two hours before we came as a group, the energies which were quiet for a while started to act up. Jack told of a phone call he received where there was only the crackling on the other end. I felt joyous. When I walked by the house where I felt the little boy watching me on the balcony, I heard him say, "The ravine, look into the ravine, there is something in the ravine."

I brought Lyn over to meet them a few days later and she confirmed the little boys' presence and also his desire to move on into the light. There was an accident that took his life in the ravine. Tonight, we are planning to go back to Jack and Karen's to hold the space for he needs to move on. I feel a strong presence of a woman that maybe his mother who will come and take him over to the light this evening. A great sense of gratitude and celebration is in the air.

It gives me great joy to share this part of the journey. When we all gathered at Jack and Karen's we shared some energy and felt the boy's presence with us. He was standing on the settee and the two cats that lived there came into the room. Karen placed them in another room because one of the women had some fear around felines. The dark cat managed to re appear and went over to the settee where the boy began petting her. A cool breeze came from his direction which is how Spirit or energy shows itself. His name was Colin, Irish descent and he said it was Jan 12th, 1906. His family had come out from St. John's Newfoundland to mine and make a living. The mother died as they were crossing the prairies.

Some of the travel was done on the train, horse and cart, then walking. The journey took them along while to get here. He appeared to be 10-12 years of age. He stood quite small with short blond hair and rag a muffin looking clothes like an Oliver character from the movie. His nickname was Cookie. I had heard a few days ago Carl as a name, so I knew I was starting to become clearer in the info. I was picking up.

An event happened that day where he was in charge of making sure no coal fell off the carts as they traveled slowly down the track. He shared that when a piece fell he would place it in his pocket and bring it home for his family to use. That day as the carts were being sent down the tracks they started to wobble, Cookie tried to steady them with his arm. The next thing he was aware of that he was falling backwards. He remembered not wanting to hit anything as he fell and that is the last of his memories. He has had the sensation of falling ever since. The coal cart toppled over top of him apparently and he died. When we visited on the last Thursday as I walked by the lower balcony I heard him ask me to look into the ravine. I knew there was a piece of information there.

He was drawn to be in Jack's house because of the coal miners lamps he had on his mantelpiece.

He was aware of a difference between us and him and asked what that was about. Lyn mentioned to him that his energy had changed. She used that term rather than dying. He was frightened because he felt he would get in trouble and had to get back to take the coal to his dad. We gently and lovingly held some energy for him. Lyn asked him to allow himself to fall again and we would catch him as a group. He still had some fear around the fall.

Soon his guide came in, a beautiful strong energy, then his mother. He turned to this unconditionally loving energy of the divine mother and heartfelt emotions were present. He couldn't believe his mother was there because she had died. He was so relieved to see her. He looked back at us to know he was somewhere other than in 1906.

Lyn noticed that the golden cord between him and his mother was not solid and asked that we envision it as complete so he could go to her. We did and sure enough he was going towards her looking back with a final glance. Then it was like the curtain was drawn. Lyn remarked how it was an emotional re union. All of us in the group felt the joy and tear filled connection.

We took a moment to re balance our energies and come to a place of peace and sharing.

I asked how they saw the mother because I wanted clarification as to the woman who connected with me in my condo. Jack expressed he saw her with dark shoulder length hair with a long skirt and a barrette, Lyn agreed.

It was she. Lyn commented on how she was part of the manifestation of this re union as well as seeing that we, as a group, were there to help. It was a wonderful feeling to know that she connected with me for help. I live across the valley, as I said, from where this all took place and this morning I glance across the valley and could feel no pull or energy there.

I bless their journey together and with gratitude bless them for the experience and conscious awareness it has brought to me.

Margaret Joan Byrd 1919- 24

We had another adventure with our development group on Sunday. We heard that a man who used to spend some time visiting a specific graveyard created an attachment to a grave plot that hadn't been kept up. This was a young girl's plot. He projected aloneness on this grave and when he moved from the small town he decided he would take a part of the stone. He always had it in a respectful place in his abode and never told anyone about it until he felt drawn to return it last week. He didn't have any experiences with the energy.

The group was asked to attend because the film group in doing this documentary of his story wanted some feedback by a medium.

We all arrived on this sunny day. The three individuals stood at the gates waiting for us.

We greeted the group and knew instantly who the person was that had returned the stone, the day before.

When we arrived at the plot a great joy and celebration of energy was there. A bubbly young expressive energy with reddish brown hair and freckles greeted us. She was delightful. The group went quiet to connect and then share in what they picked up.

Outside of her appearance, Lyn received information around who she was and how she passed over. Her mother was with her in the plot. Her father was a prominent figure in the small town possibly a lawyer or judge. She was dressed in her Sunday best, a pinafore and beautiful braids with ribbons the same color of her dress. She died of the measles quite suddenly.

The father moved from this small town to another home. His energy was not present in the grave.

In addressing pre determined contracts, they young girl came in to touch base with the Third Dimension briefly then leave. She is still felt to be happily in Spirit and not intending to come back. Margaret through this man's journey has popped in on him to see what he was up to or where he was periodically but had definitely moved on with no attachment to the plot or stone.

It was beautiful to experience that simplicity and joy in Spirit.

As we moved into the sun to continue our discussion with the crew, Lyn picked up on a nick name. Maggie Byrd. Maggie is our little magpie. It seemed like she loved nature and animals and would collect little things as Magpie's do.

We touched base with the crew on the universal understanding of death and dying. That energy changes and is never wasted, was where the conversation went next. Education is so integral to the teaching and understanding, removing the fear around the process of continuing as energy and light. The crew was moved and excited at what they had experienced. They mentioned that they would give us copies of their project when it was complete.

The book "Universal Stretches" is off to a publisher for review. Lyn and I spent the day together in meditation about three times. At around 4 pm we felt some tension around our solar plexus and wondered what we were picking up. It felt like a large energy, like some event was happening on the Earth. I lay down as I felt myself go out of my body. Within seconds Lyn was out as well. The next morning, we learned that at 5:30 pm Mountain Time, Mount St. Helen's erupted.

When I worked on Lyn in the morning to help her re balance in quiet meditation with the eternal Ohm's playing. I had a vision of an ancient time where I was sounding the tinshaws as I was sounding them up her charkas, walking up her body in ceremony. As I held energy standing by her side Angel, my healing buddy and feline friend selectively sat on her lower charkas. I saw the word Africa. When I receive information like that I just file it away. Later on that day as Lyn and I were experiencing the same discomfort I mentioned to her that Africa came to me in the morning meditation. We had no idea until later the following day a quake had killed 47 miners and 840, I believe were being rescued in Africa.

I live in, a once upon a time, mining town. It only closed down, to my surprise, in 1975. Many deaths from accidents or the Earth caving in are common here. Houses that are built on some of these energies, have the energies still present in their environment. In one of the newer developments, a road caved in. Luckily, only one vehicle was involved.

Create flow, allow yourself to get the first word or image out then trust in the experience. Know the Universe communicates to us in a myriad of ways. We need to have the basic understanding of opening our minds to receive, so the energy or communication can freely flow within us.

If it is to clear any constrictive thoughts try, mantra singing or listening to ohm's, to calm and have peace in our minds. Focusing on the mountain or tree and ask for clearing and calming is another way, breathing gently, conscious of its pathway in our bodies. That is all that is important in this moment. Let everything else fall away reaching out in all directions creating space peace and nothingness.

In this moment, I am experiencing a bubbling up of joy I own the joy and acknowledge it, receiving it in my heart. I recognize that frequency to be my connection with my higher self. When I am there I can allow myself to reach into that universal connection and access what I need to manifest in this lifetime. Be it the colors of healing, the gold thread of wisdom, white and gold light of peace, the violet and gold, green light of healing and rebalancing, the blue light of understanding and integrating information.

"The Secret" is an empowering movie which teaches us about "the Universal Law of Attraction" regarding self-healing and manifestation.

Flashes of Energy

I acknowledge the flashes of light that I see through out the day of green, violet and gold, as energies or beings that are present with me.

When I am specifically working on certain clients I will see a spark over their body or the area I am working. I trust that healing has occurred. It is a sign for me. When I am meditating and need re assurance that what is being created is on track I will usually see these sparks of lights. I don't see an orb hovering anywhere, for me is sparkles of light. I bless all my unseen friends; you unconditional love me supporting my walk here on the mother Earth planet. The compassion I feel, cushions any fear or self doubt.

For sometimes in waking I have fear and I am not sure what that is about. As soon as I feel that frequency of connecting, I become calm and ask that the light of the Universe always be with me. I bless my journey and all those I will meet today and work with, in the joy filled celebration of being here. The miracles I experience are meant to happen. It is not my ego. Opening the space for it to happen in my heart I know that certain connections occur for purpose.

There have been those I have met on my journey that have been profound relationships. These connections are there to teach or help me on my way. All is intended, as the script has already been written.

Doors will open through others that will simply assist us. Blessing that role I move on with acknowledgement.

I am always titillated how the Universe communicates to me beyond the knowing of my dreams. If I am to spend any effort in trying to second guess how it will come to me, I have missed it. That is when I hear my guidance say, "Be in the moment. Breathe. Be present in the moment."

The Owl and the Bowl

As I wander this morning, I found myself at Kim's house. She was in one of the Intuitive groups. Roberta Flack was sounding on the stereo, such heart music. I see a Tibetan bowl on the table where I had placed mine, in the class, a few nights before. I remarked on it. She expresses how it was not sounding right for her. I hold the Tibetan bowl, connecting with that higher aspect of myself and ask the bowl what it may need. I see the atoms of metal not in alignment. I ask it what I can do for it. I see it in the Earth buried for a few days. Celtic sea salt placed in it to help cleanse the energy of the person that made it. I also ask the Universe to bring through me the energies. I see and feel the violet, gold and then some green or turquoise. I ask the Universe for its love, compassion, wisdom, protection and clarity. I tell Kim, I often feel a gentle shower or energy like a waterfall flowing through me upon evoking the universal energies.

When we work with a personal bowl, the sound will evolve and start to change. I know that my bowl will make different sounds pending on the person it is treating and what is needed to be done. I have seen it clear energy and stimulate tissue, aligning the communication of hormones in the body. Kim then told me a story of one night when the cats were outside and she heard a cry. Another wild bunny, she thought. She went outside and saw some eyes under one of her trees. She thought, Alien. She walked over to find a gray owl. As she approached it, the owl spread its wings and flew away. She turned to me and said, "That is where I will place the bowl." "Beautiful," I replied. We responded in the moment to the guidance we were given. In leaving, I said, if it still doesn't resonant with you, you have had a great awareness around the bowl. You are preparing it for its next owner. If it doesn't sound right, I would return it and open yourself to receive another. She also shared how in Portland the bowl stores which are numerous were always closed, when she got there. She let go of buying one there and felt at peace knowing her home town of Canada, would bring one to her.

It will be lovely to see how this journey unfolds for her, blessings to you, my friend.

Water Work Healings with
Jay Paul and Red Hawk

Two summers ago, when I started my journey on the waters off the coast of Vancouver Island, little did I know I was connecting with an aspect of myself since the beginning of time on this planet, Lemuria.

Lyn, Red Hawk, Jay Paul, Aly, Kristina, Willy, Janet, Neil, have found each other in this small mountain town. We have come together, as we have through time, as the planet changes occur. We help anchor in energies that support this process from the spiritual Universe. That is another story of its own, but I want to focus on what was an experience for me. When I met my sailing friend Bill, he was so accommodating and insistent on Aly and me coming out on the boat. I never thought of myself as a sailor. I bought my tickets to get us out to the ocean and from then on, I never looked back. I have always felt supported in my journeying out on the ocean waters.

Before Aly and I went on our holiday, we were given a meditation to do where Jay Paul, would send some energy through us to harmonize and re balance the water. He described how it would unfold. The events of what mammals would come forward. I was preparing myself by doing the clear light meditation and the universal heart meditation, which I will share with you now.

Take a deep breath in and exhale letting go of any resistant energy that maybe in your systems. Inhale filling all your cells with Flowers and as you exhale focus on the word Fresh. Thich Nhat Hanh in his "Art of Mindful Living" CD refers to our flower wilting when we are not taking care of ourselves. By focusing on this breath for two or three days, one will feel rejuvenated.

As I am writing this, Angel, my cat, wants to come and lie on my lap. It is truly a beautiful reflection and affirmation that the energy is right for sharing this.

She prefers to lie at my feet which are comforting. I believe the Universe speaks to us in many ways; it is listening with our whole being that is the key. The diligence is to make it our daily practice.

She is now sitting beside the computer screen. I hope you can open your hearts to appreciate being in this present moment.

As you are still breathing focusing on the flower and exhaling on "fresh," I trust you are feeling centered and at peace.

Now journey into your minds eye, the center of your pineal gland, if you have that awareness, great, if not, focus within your minds eye on a single cell. Radiate your light out in all directions, the vastness and expansiveness of who we all are. Allow it to flow beyond your minds capabilities. Stretch it further than you have known, for we have been all things. Once you are there, in this moment, allow it to implode on itself the energy of all earthly experiences coming in on itself and reaches up higher than we consciously have been aware, into the clear light, the higher aspect of ourselves, where we are light and energy.

Once in that place, allow the expansiveness to extend out in all directions. Feel the vastness, color, release the physical, for you are in the place where you are light and energy. That is our original nature. Allow yourselves to float on that universal wave, the fabric of the Universe, which we draw on for assistance for what we need in this Dimension. Imagine you are that brilliant sun surrounded by a million suns. Take a few moments.

I want you now to find the mother Earth planet from where you are. Once you have her in your minds eye; with your universal heart, that place of nurturing and creation, send a ray of violet and gold light towards the planet. Be aware of how large or small the planet looks like from where you are. Be aware of the planets you are passing. As this light enfolds on this planet hold the energy there. Still be aware of your expansiveness of light in all directions. This always feels to me like a laser beam focused with intention on this planet. Breathe, opening that expansiveness of the universal heart feeling enormous love and compassion for her. It is a consciousness, a sentient being. Open yourselves to feel what she is telling you. In this moment you can choose to keep this connection running 24/7, or you can chose to withdraw your connection until the next time you enter into this meditation. There is no right or wrong whatever you are guided to do. For those that chose to continue this constant support. Trust and know it is there.

From this same place, bring your awareness into your universal heart. Breathe in and out several times experiencing the peace of who you are. Being in our truth should be as peaceful and loving. Take a few moments to fully recognize and bathe in this frequency of peace, so you can draw on it when needed. Now allow yourselves to come back slowly into the physical body. Gently and with ease, wiggle your toes and slowly open your eyes.

For those that chose to keep the energy running from that place of the universal heart, I would like you to do this meditation daily. When you are walking down the street as you look up to the sky, take note how you feel and what you see.

After I had been diligently doing this meditation for several weeks, one day I looked up and I felt the violet and gold energy raining down on me. I had the experience of being aware of myself up in the clear light at the same time as walking down the street. It was an experience that stretched my conception of multi Dimensional aspects of me. It started to open me up to a whole different awareness. Blessings to you for what you allow yourself to experiences. In opening your heart, your truth is revealed.

I going to jump into the next meditation Jay Paul took me on to tune me into experiencing the Fifth Dimensional frequencies before my trip.

Take a few moments to bring yourself into that place of clear light where the rays are extending out to the planet Earth.

Once you are there you are aware of the sun rising on the horizon of this beautiful planet. In watching the sun come from the horizon, its light connects with yours and dances in communication. This sun's rays light up the Earth. You notice that some places are dark, there are shadows present and the light does not reach all places. In the shadows, there is no growth. With tenderness, allow the day to unfold over a city and watch until the sun sets for it is now time to rest and heal from the activity of the day.

As your light, is embracing the Earth in love and compassion, the new day dawns. This time when the sun rises you notice that the rays of the sun are violet and gold, blue and silver an array of colors fill the sky. With this sun, no place is left unlit. This sun's light touches all places and there is growth everywhere. In this new day, there is no need to travel out onto the ocean for the waters are healed. There is no need to place your hands on those who are sick, because all is healed. There is no disease or famine for there is enough for all. There is balance and harmony in all things. The energy is of joy, celebration and peace. The air is light and free.

Allow yourself in your universal heart to experience this new day. When you are ready allow yourselves to slowly with ease and grace, come back into your physical body.

When Jay Paul talks about the Fifth Dimensional frequency it is that same energy. Our original nature is of that frequency. Karma does not exist in this frequency. Being in our original nature here, on Earth, is the experience. For our spirits to express themselves fully in the limitation of the Third Dimension, is the dance. The freedom to live, speak and create in this environment is the largest learning curve. It is difficult, for we experience the emotions of pain, suffering and loss. In our original nature, emotions are not part of the experience in the same way. For when we truly hold love and compassion for all, there is no space for hate, jealousy or ego.

Healing separation

The art of seeing yourself in all you meet. If we hold the understanding, that I am you, you are me and we are all one, how can I do harm to you. I can only love you and bless you with the prosperity and abundance that I truly know is our innate right. We were not put here to be in this extremity of density. The human mind has created the ego and its separation. It is now time to remember the truth and lift the veil that I am God and that this is an illusion. Seeing everyone and everything as perfect will transform the density. That is the purpose of a lot of our journeys to being Masters of bringing the light into the darkness, as we have done before.

Ackasha

www.azuritepress.com (exploring frontiers of self, science and spirituality)

Protection is very integral to this work.

I was going through a period where I kept hearing "protection" and feeling uneasy about the events around me. These emotions of fear are pulling me of my center. I think at times I am going crazy. I ask for insight and guidance. Sometimes, I am not hearing anything.

When I went to Qi Gong with Dr. Steven Aung I was reminded of the beauty of myself. He held the resonance for me to come back into balance. In 1996, I sat after hip replacement surgery in his Buddha room. He was gifted by the Dalai Lama with 8 healing Buddha's. I was surprised and excited to see that he had created a booklet of the Buddha's with his journey to Darasalama.

The first 4 Medicine Buddha's mantras were about protection. Protection for healing but also when one devotes oneself to reaching their potential, in teaching and healing themselves on all levels, that raises their level of intent. There is a protection Buddha for that as well. In the 4th Buddha, it acknowledges that there maybe some influences from maligned planets, demons or Spirit that can affect our protection as well. It was a wonderful way the Universe gave me some stronger tools to increase my protection. I was feeling shaken and unsafe. I am human.

May all the blessings be upon me May all the divas protect me By the protective power of all the Buddha's,

May safety ever be mine

This mantra is from the Buddha for "Cultivation and Teaching of Spiritual Healing Energy"

Page 18 in Dr. Aung's, "8 Medicine Buddha's"; you can purchase it off his website www.aung.com

Wildlife Greetings

I feel open and blessed with the sunny skies all around me and the colors of blue, white and the green of the trees embracing me. As I arrived home, driving out of the city a hawk flew over the car. It was right overtop of us with wings majestically spread, the tail caught the sunlight and the gentle red affirmed for me, I was home. Red Hawk blessed me. The Universe communicates to me through the wildlife I experience. A peace came over me and I felt safe. I was home. I felt a quiet gentle gratitude to call this beauty, home. I had never dived into the depths of that feeling. It was so profound the honor I experienced.

It has been two days now since I have been here and the energy within me feels heightened. The phone is ringing for appointments and I feel like I am flying through the day. Effortlessly meeting all those I need to.

Bringing Red Hawk Home

My friend, Willy had just come out of the hospital and I went to visit. Instantly upon seeing him I knew he should go back to the hospital to get checked as his first night out was traumatic and his stitches were oozing. The pain medication needed to be altered. He dressed and we made our way down the stairs through the living room when I noticed a Red Hawk on his wall.

Excitedly, I turned to him and said," Do you know who you have there?"

He said, "Yes would you like it. Someone gave it to me because he didn't know what to do with it."

My mouth dropped open. I walked gingerly over to the bird. I took him off the wall and the energy running through and around me was titillating. I couldn't believe it. A lady present who is very sensitive to energy commented on how I was buzzing.

I carried him into the car with me and proceeded to climb the stairs to my condo. Where will he go? I was shown in a brief flicker of an image; it was on the wall in the living room. Perfect.

My cat Angel was eyeing Red Hawk so I let him rest on a high shelf in my bathroom.

Red Hawk is my gate keeper guide. He has come in with me in Spirit as a primary guide and will see me through when I pass over. What I am noticing in a primary guide is that the energies are shared. There are many desires and what I enjoy mirror his interests. For example, being involved in the theatre since I was 8 years old I always had a passion for masks. I remember being a drama specialist with the Parks and Recreation Department when I was only 13 years old and doing activities such as mask making with the children. To this day, I have a collection of feather masks on my wall. When I clear and practice non attachment I haven't been able to part with these yet.

I discovered through my meditations and asking for more of our history or lifetime we shared together to be revealed, I realized he and I were partners and shamans together. Our relationship was one of equality in all ways. He has comforted me in those times where there has been lack of integrity and inequality in relationship. Be it, a lover, partner, or family member. I love drumming and making sounds. Singing was my first love. I remember being at church when I was 13 and singing a good old blues tune that came from my soul, "Little Baby Jesus born in Bethlehem". It always made my heart sing.

A Story of Adversity, reading the signs along the way

This event is a trip in the Gulf Islands on a Fast Passage which is a forty foot circum navigational sailboat. I spent 4 yeas learning to sail this vessel. It had in the past brought me many lessons and great strength. I was with Angel, Aly and our friend, Captain Bill.

As I take a deep breath in, I wonder how I am going to paint this picture of adversity, into opportunity. When we left the dock to venture out on our first day of sailing, we instantly ran into some tempest weather in the shape of hail stones. Ouch, they stung my face. I immediately thought, oh no, I don't feel incredibly supported here. What lesson or experience is in this? As we cleared the hail, the weather gave us a break until in the distance a very black wall of rain lay ahead of us. It looked like a black veil. Oh my goodness, I inhaled. I remember talking to Red Hawk, my guide, after this veil of the void, we will be okay? I wasn't enthused at my sense of the reply.

We traveled through the questionable weather unscathed.

A few days passed where now we chose to venture out on land to an ancient forest with tall red cedars that must have been 6 stories high. The beauty and majesty of the height and canopied foliage made incredible shadows with the sun streaming through.

We arrived back at the boat and I was preparing supper. I picked up Angel who was on the counter to put her on the floor. She didn't spring down like a cat would; she hit the floor with all her weight like a stone. She instantly hissed and cowered and I knew something had broken. I was emotional and went up on deck to call my friend, Lyn. With tears in my eyes, Angel made it up on deck and looked okay, as she walked around on deck. The straw that broke the proverbial camel's back was her jump, down into the 5' inside cabin of the boat. She hit the floor on her hind legs and screamed. It looked like she blew out a ligament in her knee. She hobbled around all night hiding from us. I prayed and asked that such a healing little being be given grace around this incident. I didn't want to go into the why's of all of this. It seemed absurd. The next morning we were in vicinity of a town, so I arranged to take her on land to a cat clinic. They took X-rays, gave her pain meds and sent me home with anti-inflammatories, they believed her anterior cruciate ligament was the problem, something in her knee.

This was so difficult for me. Feeling so responsible and trying to tap into the universal mind of understanding of these series of unfortunate events. A few days of hobbling around I thought taking her out on a flat surface would be gentler for her. I put her harness on and we went for a beautiful walk up and down the dock. When we got into the cabin she laid chewing on her harness, to take it off. I put my hands on the clasp and felt her teeth gently on my finger. There was no pain but a constant pressure I thought the least I can do is take it off, so I don't cause her anymore anxiety. I did and realized a few minutes later that there was blood everywhere. She broke the skin on my finger and I was bleeding. What does that mean? I had never been bitten by a cat; little did I know people have toes and fingers amputated from the deadly bacteria that are in cat's mouths.

Well, the next morning I arose the find my whole finger puffy, soreness in the joint and unable to bend it. My whole left arm seemed to ache. I connected to guidance and saw that there was some possible blood infection. I decided after much confusion to go to the Walk-in Clinic. I met with a compassionate female doctor who said with urgency that I needed to take powerful antibiotics for 14 days.

I was just coming off of the parasite recovery with all this great intestinal food I had been taking and now the thought to pollute it with anti-biotic, I cried. I felt beaten, small and my thoughts were pulling me to get off this planet. The urgency was strong to go home. Not necessarily my physical home but home, home to the creator. Giving Lyn another desperate call she assured me the anti-biotic were needed and I was to take them right away.

In reflection, I know this wasn't about me suffering through some dramatic removal of my finger. If it was to balance the energy or Karma involved with hurting Angel, I was at peace with that.

Previous to going on this adventure when Lyn and I were in the end of sending off the book "Universal Stretches" to a few people, I expressed to her my concerns about the journey and felt there was something untoward that was to occur. I was even going to cancel the trip. She felt intuitively that there was something regarding Bill's health.

I wondered whether Angel may have picked up the negative energies rather than one of us suffering with it. In talking to Lyn she shared with me that cats or animals primarily pets have the ability to do that.

I took Angel to Dr. Dave at home and he confirmed that the lateral ligament was torn and needed surgery, a type of reconstruction, for this rarely happens naturally in cats. I suspected that. I felt comforted in this decision.

I also knew that the money for this operation was going to be manifested. I wasn't going to fall into old patterns of fear but trust in the universal support. Captain Bill came through to cover 60% of the cost of the operation. I was deeply moved again at how the Universe helps and supports us. Tears came to my eyes, as I talked to him.

I know he has a difficult time with emotions, so I honored that. I did not allow myself to release the joy-filled tears but told him in honesty, how I felt. I shared that I was moved and thanked him with deep gratitude. He loved to have the opportunity to help.

So here I sit after a beautiful meditation, seeing the healing colors of green and violet grace my inner vision. Angel lay beside me, in the zone, across my lower abdomen stretched out with such amazing warmth and healing energy for her and for myself.

Red Hawk graces now my home as I write this lesson and the gifts of support flow into my heart from the Universe expressed through others around me.

I had to be disciplined not to go into old places or thought patterns imagining the awful ways this drama could have turned out. I stayed strictly in the moment of gratitude and allowed the Universe to write the story. It amazes me always how the grace and ease or peace of this played out. I bless it and all those who created this. I am blessed and full of this gentle gratitude to call this splendor home.

I had spent some energies wondering about moving on from here but the message I get from this is to be in the moment fully so that life and its many opportunities can present themselves. Otherwise, I will miss it.

Working with Willy, asking for the vortex of universal healing that is anchored in this area of the world which is just outside both of our bedrooms, to grace us by flowing into our sacred spaces and vehicles for healing. Singing Narayani mantras, blessing the wounds, balancing the brain with the trauma so the cells can start to be at peace and communicate, burning incense to keep the denser energies at bay and for cleansing through the lungs which are related to the large intestine in Chinese Medicine. These are ways we brought about healing the Spirit and the body from his adversity.

Sharing the knowing and holding the space for grieving and moving on, coming into the knowing that this created experience was to deepen ones own power and balance old energies of Karma. Realizing the power isn't in the sacred peace pipe or gemstones but that he is the pipe and gemstones. Drawing on the God creator energy that he truly is, helped his awareness. We tend to reach out to find healing, rather than go inside in these vulnerable moments.

Human Guides

The love and compassion from the Universe is nonjudgmental. We simply experience. We choose. As we have been guides for others in between human incarnations we have gently and lovingly stood by with compassion holding a space for our partners in the physical world to choose and that is all. Sometimes the Universe or Spirit intervenes, I am told. That will come in another book.

As I look up at the sky today I can see the infinite space that we live in of our physical Universe. I wonder what the spiritual Universe that runs parallel to this looks like. All I can see is color, the vibrant alive colors that radiate health and healing.

When I work or in meditations with myself, I will often go into the clear light and connect sending different vibrations for healing. Sometimes I ask that my higher guidance do that for me, as I am learning to be conscious about my process. I realize now that peace, love, compassion, balance and harmony are all frequencies as well that can be asked for, in our healing.

After the event with Angel I found I got home focusing on "Be at Peace" repeating in my head. I started feeling each cell open to this vibration letting go of resistant energy that had been caught causing pain.

Since then I have been more aware of what I ask for.

Johnston's Landing Retreat, B.C

Qi Gong

Qi Gong a profound piece of my journey, the beauty of the breath the innate power within us that we can work with to heal ourselves. Qi Gong is referred to the medical breath. The breathing is used to help rebalance and harmonize one's various meridians supporting organs and their excess or depletion. I connected with Dr. Stephen Aung in 1996 after undergoing 2 total hip reconstructions in that same year. I continue to study with him. I honor him as one of my spiritual teachers.

I flew out to his clinic to be treated and attended my first level of Qi Gong. I have been practicing the 4 breaths since then, assisting myself and clients with symptoms and correcting primary causes of dysfunction in the body.

I facilitated a Qi Gong group for a year and a half. and also introduced Qi Gong in an independent school.

The key is teaching our children, by empowering them to shift energies when needed throughout their day.

Dr. Steven Aung and Karen, Level 2 Chi Gong, June 2006

I spoke of four breaths: Simple Yin/Yang and Reinforcing Yin/Yang. There is an oxygenation breath, working with the lung. There is a breath that is detoxifying, one for emotional purification, cleansing that releases carbon dioxide and impurities from the various organs. The hand and feet positions all support the flow of energy that is generated.

As a discipline of the mind, I have used this as a form of pain control. I use accumulated Qi to shift or open the tissues or to harmonize congestion allowing for the flow of Qi and fluids to balance and restore function.

Daily practiced it keeps the skill in tune for when crisis occurs. In this world where so many external factors are at play it adds to my vitality and strength amidst the stressors of our present world.

In exploring, I found my desired way of being to blossom in intuitively whether I am at the office or at home.

I love the simplicity of the breath and truly know from my life experiences, it is a key to wellness...naturally. I urge you to send away for the level one booklet and give yourself permission to take control of your health in this simple way. www.aung.com

White, white, whiteness fills the gentle valley. I look over at the Three Sisters here in Canmore and project my energy to where I was yesterday. It is blessing the Earth with its gentleness and profound compassion. The mountains dressed in their gowns of white are a beautiful reminder for me of purification and the simplicity of white.

Sacred Places

This powerful and magical place, I first experienced with Dr. Aung and the Qi Gong class. As a group, we made our way with peace filled walking. Holding the resonance of peace as our feet touched the Earth. We are peace. At the base of the mountain, we had our meditation and ceremony.

Since then, I have taken many people there to experience the frequencies and healings. Other sentient beings, the eagle, the sheep, a few ravens and the first spring's running water would make themselves known.

This sacred place was calling to me. I felt guided that my friend Willy was to come this time with me. As we made our way with excitement, we stopped first at my home. I introduced him to Angel and some of my crystals that have come into my life over the past few years.

He was standing in the window facing the Three Sisters I was drawn to a Russian Citrine. I gave it to him to hold and the energy shifted around him. It was like a reunion. We looked at each other and laughed, we just knew it had to come to the vortex with us. We wrapped it up in a towel and it sat with Willy as we journeyed there.

I asked permission as we were about to make our way at the bottom of the mountain for the support of the Universe with its love, protection and direction. I held a space open for whatever needed to manifest. It was an effort to clear my mental mind of all my other experiences and be in the magic of the present moment.

We gently climbed the hill as Willy shared his knowledge of the native ingredients for smudge that was here. The pussy willows had broken through the skins and the soft white buds were peeping out as if to say "Hello."

As we reached the walkway to the base, the Wind howled, the Trees spoke to us in their voices. It was a powerful Wind. We stopped in our tracks. When the Wind and Trees finished we continued on our way understanding permission was granted. The sun followed in blessing us with its light and heat. We acknowledged the gift by stopping spreading our wings to receive "yes."

Slowly with joy our physical bodies were showing signs of experiencing a change in vibration. Willy began to sweat and I felt giddy. Arriving at the base of the mountain we found a rock to sit on and entered into meditation. Willy placed the Russian Citrine at our feet on the Earth.

Willy and I shared some powerful energy and the experience originally was to be open to receive clarity around that energy we share. He removed his socks and shoes so that his feet could be one with the Earth. I began with the breath and a blessing asking that my heart be open to receive and invite healing on any level needed. I closed my eyes and was drawn into the cosmos. At that moment, I felt other energies and then I saw a brilliant luminescent Willy joy filled. There were other energies present but they didn't need to be in form. They were highly evolved beings of brilliant light sending energy. This energy was coming down through us into the Earth.

The compassion I felt, took me into a new depth of that frequency. I find as I grow, my love or how I define that love, deepens and the frequency gets finer tuned. The citrine stood at our feet. The triangle of our energies felt beautiful.

I was drawn to walk where a large boulder, the size of me, stood. I walked up to it, wrapping my arms around it. Closing my eyes, I was transported into space with the image of holding the Earth in a big hug and the waves of compassion moved through me, I began to weep. I began to feel I am the Earth weeping. When the energy of love and compassion was complete, it was clear like a tap, which had stopped. I separated from the boulder with humble gratitude and made my way back.

I found Willy kneeling in quiet prayer. It was gentle and beautiful.

It is done. It is done. It is done.

We knew in our hearts it was time to go.

With joy and laughter, we shared our feelings.

We chose another route down the mountain, before we had walked the path. The Wind came up again and the trees roared. We stopped and acknowledged its message. I felt it was in celebration and gratitude for being there, like a roaring crowd in rock concert. We found some soft grass that cushioned our weight. We continued to walk with laughter and awe of this gift then we lay in gratitude, supported by the Earth.

The art of truly being in the present moment, where the moment past and in front of us, is irrelevant. In this moment life is "pretty great". The expansiveness of the valley filled with nature's beauty, blankets of evergreens and mountains are with us, all the greens, whites, browns, blues, reds and gold all around and beneath us.

The splendor of pussy willows beside us invites Willy to take some home. He offers tobacco and then proceeds to carefully pick the branches that offer themselves to him. He turns to me and hands me a gift of pussy willows. He picks a few for himself. It is amazing how mine had beautiful female energy and his was definitely male. The bark had different colors of red and brown. He also picked one for Angel.

Journeying home he knew that the Three Sisters would look different to us after having this experience.

Fortress Mountain, AB, Canada

How many of us are guided to go out in nature and truly respond to the call. In nature, there are so many ways to come closer to our truth and healing. To balance and bring into harmony for ourselves in this busy world that seems its purpose at times is to pull us off our centers. Give yourself permission to receive the wonders and compassion that nature has for you. Truly, we are not judged in that place, but find the peace in our hearts that fuel us home into our reality.

I have another sacred place that I go to for a quick connection with nature, by my office. I was walking and was drawn to the Earth beneath me. The connection I make every time I take a step. The focus then shifted to my head and crown. The energy that comes from the higher aspect of me flows down getting anchored in the physical experience through my body which is my connection with the Earth. My transmitter is my physical body. This is where the frequencies and gifts I have come into this lifetime with are manifested.

In this moment, take a deep breath in and exhale. Take another breath in and exhale again, clearing any resistant energy, bring yourself into the center of who you are. When you are there, focus your awareness at your feet. Feel the energy moving through you into the Earth. Now take your attention to the clear light place of peace where the energies come into you from the spiritual Universe. Open your heart to receive the knowing of the spiritual and physical Universe. A miracle of how we continually are connected to the two. This is how I bring the spiritual Universe into the physical Universe. This can begin to expand our awareness of our multi Dimensional levels of being. How we can be conscious of relationships that exist on other levels of our being at the same time. These are a few concepts to meditate on.

In the vortex experience, the transmitters of who Willy is and I am at that moment, is how these energies can be sent through us, to others and the Earth, to help heal and shift the consciousness of humanity. That is why sometimes only standing near someone; we have the "Yes" feeling.

I was told by Jay Paul, that it might be as simple as walking by a person on the street, which is part of our contract. The simplicity is beautiful. On other levels, we maybe exchanging energy which may help us shift our understanding or reality. We are so busy doing. It is in the being and trusting our hearts that we truly listen and receive direction.

There is one other time I have felt this universal compassion. It was when Jay Paul, Aly with myself where doing a specific meditation with the ocean and mammal energy. As I placed my hand in the water, this immense love and compassion came through me, as if I was holding the waters of the Earth in my heart. He told me in the meditation, he would be sending this energy for healing through me at that time. I feel blessed and full of joy to be of assistance on this physical plane. I had the image of the mother caressing her child, sending her such love that would transform and heal all wounds.

Heart Rock Meditation

As I venture out for a hike or a meditative walk I open my heart in sending to the Earth that Universal Love and compassion with each footstep. With that intention the colors brighten with luminescence and glow around me, notice for yourself how the environment changes. In being present with this wonderful energy I begin to see a reflection of the energy I am holding. Rocks in the shape of hearts start to appear before me. I stop and acknowledge each one with a smile on my face. I have a deep desire to take them all home with me. I leave them on my path for others to discover them.

In the beginning, I couldn't believe the profoundness of this simple meditation. I did take a few home and also to my office. The rocks that sat on my table in my office became teaching tools for the children and those that needed to learn of this walk. For the children, it was like a game and the adults that it touched became a focus for change.

In truth, connecting with our environment will reflect our original nature. We tend to always find peace there, rebalancing ourselves.

Policeman's Creek, Canmore, AB, Canada

This heart showed up in the water as I was taking pictures for this book. I am not sure whether there was a heart shaped rock or a gift of a water reflection. I open my heart to receive and know without a doubt, Mother Earth is generous.

Heart Rock Monument, Spray Lakes, Alberta

When I was a child I felt that if I walked slowly enough, I would disappear. As I walk today, I embrace that knowing with purpose walking, truly feeling my energy in connection with the Earth. Soon I start to feel the yummy massaging of my feet as they press into the Earth. Each step another muscle and tendon experience the beauty of touch.

Policeman's Creek, Canmore, Alberta, Canada

I walk along the river feeling the energy of the trees and stillness of the mountains their magnificent presence. I am fully aware that the river is a flowing mighty fast for my pace. I focus on the connection with the Earth. This is the connection with our original nature our soul family and ourselves in physical form meet. In this interface, I easily with grace experience our oneness.

Banff, AB, Canada

As the appropriate bench comes into view facing the sun, I sit. Breathing in, out, holding my breath I do the Fourth breath in Qi Gong. I place my hands in front of me and do the blessing from the sixth Medicine Buddha.

Let those who are in misery be free from misery

Let those who are in fear be free from fear.

Let those who are in sorrow be free from sorrow

Let all sentient beings be free from misery, fear and sorrow

I do this 3 times.

Breathing in with stillness then expanding my energy at the dantian, our power center.

The quiet, outside of the rushing river, envelopes me and I hear,

The Earth is a creation of love

You are a creation of love

As you let this love, this frequency, flow through you, out into the world, it will come back to you.

I then saw the many images representing how it comes to me, as dear friends, abundance, and a home, an occupation I love and support financially. These create a myriad of images that flow through my mind's eye.

I recite this phrase that was given to me to anchor it in my heart.

With the beauty of the fresh snow that had fallen this morning, the mountains, as I remarked, are all dressed in white. As I lift my eyes to the mountain range that is in front of me I see my love, the eagle, against the white snow of Rundle Range. I transfix my gaze and breathe in as it anchors within me this experience. I acknowledge its presence with deep gratitude and blessings, with that, it changes its course and disappears.

It is done. It is done. It is done.

Closing Blessing

As I sit holding peace in my heart, I leave you on this part of the journey. In truth, I am always with you. Angel gently makes her way onto my shoulder asking to be apart of this blessing. It makes me smile as her place in this has been beautiful. As the universal light always shines within you, may it brighten your radiance as you deepen your journey knowing that you are loved and are love. Know in your heart that others around you will be touched in many ways as you heal yourself, opening your heart to your full potential. The

Earth and humanity are experiencing that wave of understanding as well, for energy is never wasted. May you also be blessed with the ease, grace and the joy filled celebration of being here, For I Am you and you are me and we are all one.

In love and light,

Karen and Angel (meow)

Resources

Andrews, T. (1995). Animal-Speak: The spiritual and magical powers of creatures great and small. St. Paul, MN: Llewellyn Publications.

Andrews,L. (1986) Star Woman: New York: Warner Books

Andrews, L. (1993) Woman on the Edge of Two Worlds: New York: Harper Collins

Aung, S. (2000) 8 Medicine Buddhas: Edmonton: College of Integrated Medicine

Aung.,S. (1996) Aung Medical Qi Gong Volume One: Edmonton: College of Integrated Medicine

Braden, G. (1996). Awakening to Zero Point: The Collective Initiation. Bellevue,WA: Radio Bookstore Press.

Coelho, P. (1993) The Alchemist: San Francisco: HarperCollins

Emoto, M. (2004) The Hidden Messages in Water: Hillsboro, Ore.: Beyond words Pub.

Emoto, M. (2005) True Power of Water: Hillsboro, Ore.: Beyond Words Pub.

Hanh, T.N. (2001) Anger: New York: Riverhead

Hanh, T.N. (2002) No Fear, No Death: New York: Riverhead

Hanh, T.N. (1975) The Miracle of Mindfulness: Boston, Mass.: Beacon Press

Hanh, T. N. (2005). Being Peace. Berkley, CA: Parallax Press.

Hanh, T. N. (1992). Peace is every step: The path of mindfulness in everyday life. New York: Bantam Books.

Hanh, T.N. (2003) Creating True Peace: New York: Free Press

Lama, Dalai. (2002) The Spirit of Peace: London: Thorsons, HarperCollins

Lama, D. (2005). The Universe in a single atom: The convergence of science and spirituality. New York: Random House.

Martel, Y. (2001) Life of Pi: Toronto: Vintage Canada

Virtue, D. (2001). The Care and Feeding of Indigo Children. Carlsbad, CA: Hay House Inc.

Virtue, D. (1997). Angel Therapy: Healing messages for every area of your life. Carlsbad, CA: Hay House Inc.

CD

Lyn Inglis "Clear Light Meditation"

Thich Hnat Hanh "The Art of Mindfulness"

Websites

James Twyman, www.emissaryoflight.com

Dr. Doreen Virtue, www.angeltherapy.com

Lyn Inglis, www.lyninglis.com

CD's, www.soundstrue.com

Gregg Braden, www.greggbraden.com

Spiritual Cinema Circle, www.spiritualcinemacircle.com

www.azuritepress.com

Health, www.mercola.com

Indigo, www.indigoevolution.com

Karen Barker, www.karenbarker.ca

Dr. Steven Aung, www.aung.com

Narayani Amma, www.narayaniamma.org